THE CONSTITUTIONAL POLITY

*The Gaspar G. Bacon Lecture
on the Constitution
of the United States*

1968

THE

CONSTITUTIONAL

POLITY

Glendon Schubert

BOSTON UNIVERSITY PRESS

BOSTON, MASSACHUSETTS

1970

For Susan
mahalo nui loa
no ke aloha

"Our judges are not monks or scientists, but participants in the living stream of our national life."

EARL WARREN
"The Law and the Future,"
Fortune (November 1955)

The Bacon Lectureship

The Gaspar G. Bacon Lectureship on the Constitution of the United States was established in 1927 by Mrs. Robert Bacon of New York in honor of her son, at that time Secretary of the Board of Trustees of Boston University. After several terms in the Massachusetts General Court (legislature) and two years as Lieutenant Governor, Gaspar G. Bacon retired from active politics and joined the Department of Government, College of Liberal Arts at Boston University in 1938. His teaching career was interrupted by four years of service in World War II. September 1947 found Professor Bacon back at Boston University, but only for a short period which ended suddenly with his death on Christmas Day.

Since 1927 the Bacon Lectures have been given annually by an eminent scholar or jurist in fulfillment of the terms of the deed of gift which reads, "The purpose of the Lectureship is to stimulate a study of the Constitution of the United States, its antecedents, history and doctrine, together with the results and implications thereof."

PREFACE

In accepting the invitation to deliver the 1968 Gaspar G. Bacon Lecture on the Constitution of the United States, I set for myself a task that I knew would be difficult, and perhaps impossible, of accomplishment, at least by the time the lecture was scheduled for delivery. What I would have liked ideally to have done would have been to discuss a transactional view of the reciprocal relation between American constitutional symbolism and political behavior, in application to a causal model of constitutional change. Such a viewpoint implies a model in which the Constitution is a constellation of variables, and constitutional theory is stated in mathematical form as the causal laws of interaction between and among subsets of variables.[1] (One such subset, for example, might consist of nine variables representing the justices of the United States Supreme Court; another subset might include the policy values supported, positively or negatively, by the Court in its decisions.) Of course, I was quite aware that existing research studies would not even begin to support such a sophisticated and quantified analysis of constitutional change;[2] but I thought it ought to be possible to venture a

1. Edward J. Weissman, "Mathematical Models of Judicial Behavior" (Ph.D. diss., University of North Carolina, 1969); also his "Mathematical Theory and Dynamic Models" in Glendon Schubert and David J. Danelski, eds., *Comparative Judicial Behavior* (New York: Oxford University Press, 1969).

2. See my "The Rhetoric of Constitutional Change," *Journal of Public Law* 16 (1967): 16–50.

ix

sketch of some rudiments of a behavioral model of constitutional change, even though it be subject to a multiplicity of limitations due to the unevenness through time and the generally inadequate state of empirical data, theory, and methods alike.

The level of theory for which I have had to settle (assuming that the task were to be done at all within any proximate future) is simplistic—although certainly no more so than that of most other discussion of the subject. The level of methodology is crude, with virtually none of the measurement upon which I shall rely transcending first-order linear correlation, and with much of it even simpler percentage ratios or merely marginal frequencies. Yet, I console myself with the realization that even crude counting is an important step beyond the verbal counterparts of ordinal or nominal scales, or the merely idiosyncratic appraisals of unique events, upon which much previous work in the field perforce has tended to rely. The empirical data are widely variant in quality and quantity, evoking the image of a cornucopia with an abundance of present fruit but an almost vanishing point extending a half century into the past with a country headed "back to normalcy."

The assumption that underlies the theoretical structure of this book is that the selection of Supreme Court justices reflects the same basic trends in public attitudes that result in political change in the personnel and policies of the presidency and the Congress. Of course there are differences in the institutional procedures for selecting presidents, congressmen, and judges; and it is possible for the majority point of view of the Supreme Court to become either very much behind *or significantly in advance of* public opinion. Moreover, the systemic relation among the Court and the Congress and the public (and other Court clienteles) is an open and dynamic one with reciprocal feedback loops, and with the possibility that any or all of these classes of actors will learn (and therefore modify their behavior) as the consequence of past experience. One—only one, it is true, but a significant one—of the components influencing political change will be the ideologies (belief systems) of the individual Supreme Court justices, because at the level of manifest behavior it is the intersection of these individual ideologies that produces the "attitude of the Court" and its decision toward any particular issue at a discrete time. In the theory, such individual ideologies are dynamic structures, subject to modification by social interaction both on and off the Court,[3] by the quality and quantity of stimuli that are available as issues to which the Court can respond in its decisions, by the kinds of responses that are induced from others as a consequence of the Court's decisions, and by the more diffuse processes of socialization, reinforcement, and other aspects of learning that account for the construction of individual ideologies even as a priori (to the Court) and static patternings of values.[4] Clearly the theory posits a complex set of interacting processes; but in the analysis here I shall attempt to select out and focus upon only a single such process: the pattern of individual judicial ideologies of the justices, resulting in the positively correlated patterns of output values (measured by policy trends in the Court's decisions), which in turn result in differentials in awareness of and support of and compliance with the Court's policies.[5] Thus reduced to

3. And therefore explicitly subject to reconsideration when the ideological structure of the group changes, as it does (for example) whenever a personnel replacement occurs.

4. See Hans J. Eysenck, *The Psychology of Politics* (London: Routledge and Kegan Paul, 1954), Ch. 4.

5. See my *Judicial Policy-Making* (Chicago: Scott, Foresman, 1965), Ch. 5; cf. Walter F. Murphy, *The Elements of Judicial Strategy* (Chicago: University of Chicago Press, 1964), p. 32, and Thomas P. Jahnige and Sheldon Goldman, eds., *The Federal Judicial System* (New York: Holt, Rinehart and Winston, 1968), p. 4.

a single linear sequence, the multiplex curvilinear theory is simplified, perhaps oversimplified to such a degree that it should be termed (as I already have done) simplistic. But it is not naïve.

In presenting the lectures upon which this book is based, I departed from the logical sequence of even my linear theory, and discussed first outputs, then attitudes, and last responses. My reason was the assumption that it would be easier for my audience to identify with, and to follow, a presentation that focused first upon what for them would be relatively most familiar—what the Court had decided—and then moved back to pick up the judicial "inputs" before turning to questions of impact and compliance. I believe that the same consideration ought to hold for the present audience of the book; and therefore I have sacrificed chronologic to psychologic in determining the format for the three chapters.

Methodologically, it is necessary to approximate the continuous dynamic of the time dimension (of fifty years) by an incremental treatment of extended subperiods (with "Courts" averaging over eight years in length); and it is not unjustifiable to characterize an analysis based upon such large time-units as "static." Moreover, consistent measurements are *not* available for all three classes of variables (viz., judicial attitudes, decisional policy outputs, and responses to Court policies) for all six time-units of the analysis. The most consistent measurement relates to judicial attitudes, and covers the most recent five time-units (since 1930); next comes policy outputs, covering the more recent four time-units only (since 1937); and least well measured have been responses to the Court's policies, there being no really consistent data on this even for the most recent time-unit (of the Warren Court during the sixties).

Data are of course potentially available, in the Coombsian sense that records of behavior exist and are accessible for observation and classification.[6] But the traditional literature of constitutional law, constitutional philosophy, and constitutional history, having been writ large by humanist scholars, each of whom was content to "do his own thing" and let posterity worry about problems of interobserver agreement and reliability, does not readily lend itself to efforts at aggregation and synthesis. Particularly in the early sections of the first chapter, where I seek to summarize three decades of "prehistory" (i.e., of the Supreme Court's policy outputs during the period before my own analysis proper begins) and the decade of the twenties—all of which have been abundantly studied, but not from a behavioral point of view —I may well be accused of presenting more an artistic than a scientific account of the Court's work. The accusation may be well taken, and I recognize the limited possibility of bootstrapping one's data sources and methodological parameters. But at least I have tried to be explicit about the reasons for what may seem to be a disjunction between the earlier, and the middle and later parts of the book.

The lack of general, systematic, quantified studies of Supreme Court policy making during the period prior to 1937 presents a serious problem to anyone who seeks to discuss policy trends that transcend the modern (post-1937) period. One solution would be to undertake the basic research that no one else yet has published; but this is not a feasible alternative for a lecturer confronted with a deadline and other prior research commitments. Another solution would be to truncate the analysis, and stick to the modern throughway; but I was loathe to do that because of my strong conviction that 1937 is better viewed as a watershed than as a barrier sealing off the past. The third possibility, for which I opted, was to rely for data upon the nonquantified but certainly

6. Clyde Coombs, *A Theory of Data* (New York: Wiley, 1964), Ch. 1.

policy-oriented research of such eminent conventional scholars as Alpheus Mason and Walton Hamilton, checking their generalizations against my own examination and sample analyses of the raw voting and opinion data for the two decades of the Taft and the Hughes Courts. The selected procedure did not, to be sure, provide me with data of the same quality—in terms of validity, reliability, and underlying methodological rigor—as those upon which I have been able to rely since 1937, and particularly for the most recent two decades. But neither have I premised my remarks upon traditional colloquies regarding legal doctrine and opinion verbiage. It is not true that (as one advance reader has suggested) much of the first chapter is devoted to a lawyerlike rehash of case law. In lieu of any relevant descriptive statistics, I do use individual decisions to exemplify decisional policy trends. But my concern in so doing is strictly with the institutional impact of the Court through the gross pattern of outputs that I seek to trace; and I am therefore not concerned with either the doctrinal significance or doctrinal consistency of cases, nor with the propriety of their classification under other rubrics that lawyers and constitutional historians have utilized to subserve purposes different from the one that I entertain here. However inadequate the results of my pragmatic compromise (in electing to work with the best data available for the pre-1937 period) may be deemed by either traditional (legal) or empirical (political) critics, I hope that my own clumsy efforts will spur on those who are dissatisfied, impelling them to undertake the more rigorous, quantified policy analysis that is as full in scope, articulation, and rational explication as the legal analysis that it will surely replace, at least among political scientists.

Several advance readers of the book were troubled by my use of liberalism/conservatism as the basic ideological component in terms of which I have classified both judicial attitudes and Court policies. It is of course central to my purpose to have endeavored to make a consistent analysis of the entire period utilizing the same set of concepts; and I have attempted to explain, early in Chapter II, how and why a unidimensional analysis does reasonably well until 1937, and a two-dimensional analysis is essential thereafter—subject to the caveat that a more complex multidimensional analysis, if it were (as it presently is *not*) feasible, would be preferable. As applied to the policy content of Supreme Court decision making, I use the concepts "liberal" and "conservative" precisely as I have defined them operationally and employed them in previous research;[7] for present purposes I have in Chapters I and II defined "liberal" and "conservative" in terms of their principal policy/attitudinal content. In a few instances I use the concept "reactionary" but I believe that it is perfectly clear in context that what I mean is the attempt to reinstate, at some later time, what was a former conservative position that subsequently became displaced by a more liberal policy outcome. This is consistent with what is central to my use of liberalism and conservatism, which is to identify the relative extremes of challenge to and defense of the status quo, as positions within the framework of the prevailing institutional processes for consultation and accommodation of conflict between the "haves" and "have nots." In relation to that paradigm, "radicals" are persons who seek to induce or to forestall change by resorting to revolutionary tactics that bring them outside of the established institutional decision-making processes; and they may, of course, be radicals of the right or radicals of the left.[8]

7. See my *The Judicial Mind* (Evanston: Northwestern University Press, 1965), Chs. 5 and 6.
8. Edward Shils, "Authoritarianism 'Right' and 'Left' " in Richard Christie and Marie Jahoda, eds., *Studies in the Scope and Method of the Authoritarian Personality* (Glencoe, Ill.: The Free Press,

PREFACE

I have not attempted to do much in the way of distinguishing radicalism from liberalism or conservatism in the chapters that follow, because I have had no reason to do so. As I do point out, during the period of my analysis the Supreme Court has included no radicals, with a single possible (and recent) exception; nor has the Court as yet confronted very much in the way of radical issues. At least as I read them, and as I have attempted to measure them, the *United States Reports* are concerned thus far with only a pale reflection of the kinds of radical behaviors in the urban streets and on the campuses, that are reported by TV and the press—to say nothing of the much uglier events that go unreported. I can, however, suggest four dimensions—political, social, psychological, and cultural—in terms of which I think it is readily possible and appropriate to distinguish between radicalism and liberalism:

1. *Political:* Liberals believe in evolutionary change; radicals, in revolutionary tactics.

2. *Social:* Liberals are primarily from the middle class; radicals, from the leisure class.

3. *Psychological:* Liberals are tolerant of the beliefs of others; radicals are highly intolerant of each other as well as of others.

4. *Cultural:* Liberals are assimilated to the prevailing culture; radicals are alienated from it.

On the other hand, radicals share with conservatives a preference for humanism over science, and for values over facts. I have every confidence that if and when radicalism comes to the Supreme Court, the conceptual tools that I have em-

---

1954), pp. 24–49; Egon Bittner, "Radicalism," *International Encyclopedia of the Social Sciences* (New York: Macmillan, 1968) 13:294–300.

ployed herein can and will be modified so as to take into account whatever changes such an event may betoken.

In revising my lecture notes for publication, I have been assisted by several friends and colleagues who have been most generous in bestowing upon me a portion of what I am well aware is their most precious gift—professional time —by reading the book in draft and favoring me with their comments. I owe a particular debt to Martin Shapiro, professor of political science at the University of California (Irvine) for having engaged himself so deeply and extensively in my manuscript that my revision owes more to his critique than to any other single source. I was particularly assisted by the thoughtful suggestions of Sheldon Goldman, assistant professor of government, University of Massachusetts; Alpheus Thomas Mason, Doherty Professor of Government and Law at the University of Virginia; Arthur Selwyn Miller, professor of law at the National Law Center, George Washington University; and Albert Somit, chairman of the Department of Political Science at the State University of New York at Buffalo. I received helpful comments and advice from Henry Abraham, professor of political science, University of Pennsylvania; David J. Danelski, associate professor of political science at Yale University; Torstein Eckhoff, director of the Institute for Sociology of Law and Public Administration, University of Oslo; Henry Kariel, professor of political science, University of Hawaii; Fred Kort, professor of political science, University of Connecticut; Robert V. Presthus, chairman of the Department of Political Science, York University; Wallace Mendelson, professor of government, University of Texas at Austin; Jack W. Peltason, chancellor of the University of Illinois, Urbana; Geoffrey Sawer, research professor of law, Australian National University; Harold J. Spaeth, professor of political science, Michigan State University; and Edward J. Weiss-

PREFACE

man, assistant professor of political science, York University. For her careful and competent assistance in typing several drafts of the manuscript that resulted in this book, I am indebted to my secretary, Mrs. Florence Griffin. I thank Mrs. Louise Turnpenny and Mrs. Regi Reichert of the Office of Secretarial Services of the College of Arts and Sciences, York University, for their aid in reproducing copies of the manuscript for both the Bacon Lecture and this book. The book is dedicated to my eldest, and most irrepressible, daughter.

Glendon Schubert

Port Credit, Ontario
April 1969

CONTENTS

I

Constitutional Policy
Field's Legacy; Taft's Team in the Twenties;
The Nine Old Men; Economic Policy Since 1937;
Civil Liberties Since 1937.

II

Constitutional Politics
The Taft Court; The Hughes Court;
The Roosevelt Court; The Vinson Court;
The Early Warren Court—1953–1962;
The Later Warren Court—1962–1969.

III

The American Polity
Why Has the Supreme Court Changed Its Policies?
How Is the Court Constrained by the Political Regime?
What Has Been the Impact of the Warren Court's Policies?

Notes

CHAPTER I

CONSTITUTIONAL

POLICY

There is a scene early in *Through the Looking Glass*—it comes in the second chapter, and is, indeed, White Pawn Alice's very first move in the game of surrealistic chess—in which she first runs and then is pulled at top speed for an agonizing time that seems endless, handlocked tight in the grasp of a Red Queen, who (under the rules of play) is Alice's most formidable antagonist. They both have run long and hard, and gotten nowhere—or, to be more precise, nowhere *else*: the setting is the same as when they began. This surprises Alice, who remarks that in England one would have made some progress as the fruit of such an investment of time and effort. In Looking-Glass Land, however, "it takes all the running you can do, to keep in the same place." As the Red Queen explained, "if you want to get somewhere else, you must run at least twice as fast as that!" Of course, the French have an epigram to express the same point much more succinctly.[1] (An American who comes to the birthplace of Holmes and the home of Brandeis and Frankfurter, from a residence amidst our good neighbors to the North, may perhaps be pardoned if he shows what may seem to be an overweening sensitivity to the possible relevance of both British

3

whimsy and Gallic proverbs, to problems of North American constitutionalism.)

A more characteristically Yankee proposition that is both less poetic, and less clever, but may nevertheless be more profound (and useful for present purposes), is that everything changes—but with differing directions, rates, and consequences. Some things change so slowly that what we perceive, even with the aid of the best technical training and observational equipment available, is no change at all, notwithstanding our intellectual awareness throughout the present century that we inhabit a physical universe in which (at least) the *in*animate aspects of life are in continual flux.[2] Other things change so rapidly that we lose track of the continuities of metamorphic stages, leading many well-intentioned political reformers to ignore social chrysalises that offer relatively easy pickings, chasing instead after butter (or dragon) flies that offer more attractive, but difficult, targets for apprehension. Especially in our perception of political affairs, we tend to exaggerate both the permanence of institutional structures, and the idiosyncrasy of the behavior of our political elites. Such errors do not cancel each other out, although they mutually reflect, no doubt, the relative crudity of the instruments (and the associated lack of generality in the theory) with which social scientists work.[3] And because the type of professional education that makes possible scientific inquiry into social relations has come last and least to students of constitutional law and constitutional history—irrespective whether their disciplinary standpoint be that of law or history or political science—we largely continue to live in a constitutional world that tends to run to extremes.

A major task for modern social science jurisprudence is to attempt to close the large gap that necessarily obtains in our understanding of constitutional politics, when our insights are caught up in the tension between constant institutional structures and the inconstant humans who operate them. A first step in that direction is to hypothesize that the formal components of constitutional structure are themselves variables and ought to be so studied; and conversely, that the communalities and continuities in human behavior are sufficiently large so that many generalizations about the behavior of judges can be both useful and valid.[4] It is from this point of view that I should like to examine the role of the United States Supreme Court in relation to constitutional change in the American polity.[5]

In this initial chapter, I shall undertake to describe the manifest content of Supreme Court policy making during the past half century or so. In so doing I shall seek to focus upon the emergence and displacement of particular policy themes, relating these (to the extent possible) to more sweeping shifts in the climate of opinion of the Court. In particular, we shall take note of the more recent policy innovations of the Warren Court. There are several reasons for emphasizing the more recent work of the Court. It has been the subject of the most thorough and relevant research for the sort of data needed in the present inquiry. Conversely, least reliance can be placed upon what I shall say concerning the nineteen twenties, because the work on this earlier period has been almost entirely biographical, and only a few systematic studies of specialized (and none of general) scope are available.[6] A second reason for emphasizing the most recent period of the Court's work is that only under Warren did the Court emerge in splendid isolation as the most liberally oriented major policy-making group in the entire American system of government. A third reason is that the immediate past, and the present, provide the best basis for the projection of current trends into the at least short-range future.

In the second chapter I examine the ideological structure of the Supreme Court in relation to changes that have occurred in our national political leadership over the course of the past several decades.

The third chapter relates the Court's policies to their consequences for the other major political actors directly or indirectly affected by the decisions: presidents, congressmen, administrators, lower court judges, state legislators and administrators, businessmen, union officials, and the mass American public.

The scope of the book can be summarized as follows: the first chapter presents an analysis of Supreme Court outputs; the second, of inputs; and the third, of effects. The overall objective is to analyze, as dispassionately and as validly as I can, the contemporary political role of the United States Supreme Court.

Field's Legacy

In order to appraise the Court's policy making during the twenties, it is necessary to look even further back, and to examine briefly the Court's role in the decades immediately preceding. A peak of judicial conservatism, the effects of which were markedly reactionary, had been established in the early months of 1895, when in quick succession the Court first had declared the Sherman Anti-trust Act inapplicable to the industrial processes of manufacturing and production, no matter how monopolistic might be the relevant privately institutionalized arrangements for managerial direction and financial control; next it had upheld the use of antilabor injunctions by the lower federal courts in combination with President Cleveland's commitment of federal troops—and not by invitation from, but rather explicitly against the advice of the governor of Illinois—to break the Pullman strike in Chicago the previous year; and third, the Court had declared unconstitutional the income tax that Congress had enacted a few months earlier.[7] The direct consequences were to support during the next half dozen years the Cleveland and McKinley administrations in their policy of nontrustbusting; to encourage the rise a decade later of the radical and violent trade unionism of the Wobblies (International Workers of the World) by branding as illegitimate Eugene Debs's attempts to reform rather than to overthrow the existing industrial and political systems, by organizing and leading workingmen within the framework of those systems; and to postpone for a generation the adoption of a national income tax.

In throwing their support behind a by-then mature and entrenched industrial plutocracy which in order to achieve its economic and political goals needed no additional favors from the judiciary, decisions of the Supreme Court in 1895 were reactionary in effect because, at least in regard to the Sherman and income tax acts, the Court was acting to veto limited and partial reforms that had been approved by Congresses for which the Senate was at that time still chosen by state legislatures, and by presidents as devoted to the gold standard and the capitalistic system as were Benjamin Harrison and Grover Cleveland. The Court's promonopoly, antilabor, antitaxation policies of 1895 marked the ultimate, if belated,[8] triumph of the extremist laissez faire views of Stephen Field, a Lincoln appointee who had lobbied with his colleagues for over three decades to persuade them to write both *The Wealth of Nations* and *Social Statics* into the Constitution. "The present assault upon capital," Field intoned in his concurring opinion in the income tax case, "is but the beginning. It will be but the steppingstone to others, larger and more sweeping, till our political contests will become a war of the poor against the rich." [9] Now at long last Field's socioeconomic ideology was shared by a majority of the justices, including his own nephew, David Brewer; the chief justice, Fuller; Bostonian Horace Gray; and railroad lawyer George Shiras, the only Supreme Court justice who never previously had held a political position.

Field's Court heard very few appeals of any sort that raised claims to civil rights or liberties, and it is easy to understand why this was so. Claims to personal liberty tended to be made, in Field's day as in our own, on behalf of persons who are poor, not well educated, often members of what are the minority groups of the time, criminals, persons who are psychically as well as socially and economically dispossessed. The Supreme Court in 1895 did not define its political role in terms of the assurance of personal liberty for the downtrodden; quite to the contrary, it sat to guarantee constitutional liberty that could be defined in terms of property rights, and its mission was to minimize governmental interference with the sacred and anterior right of all to participate, each according to his natural advantages and disadvantages, in the marketplace that measured and rewarded the worth of them all. One of those rare cases in which that court did consider a claim to human freedom was in the now notorious and then fateful—in its implications for social relations in this country three-quarters of a century later—case in which a defendant named Plessy, seven-eights white and only an indiscernible one-eighth black, argued that segregation was unconstitutional. One might have thought that a group of men who had lived through the Civil War, and of whom eight were adults by the time Dred Scott's case was decided in 1857, would have learned something from the Court's institutional (if not from the nation's cultural) experience, as a consequence of that "self-inflicted wound." Lest we forget, it was then that Chief Justice Roger Taney, himself born on a Southern plantation to a father who was the fifth generation to work it with slaves, said of Dred Scott's claim to personal freedom that: "The question is simply this: Can a negro, whose ancestors were imported into this country, and sold as slaves, become a member of the political community formed and brought into existence by the Constitution of the United States, and as such become entitled to all the rights, and privileges, and immunities, guaranteed by that instrument to the citizen?" [10] As we all know, the Supreme Court's answer to Taney's question was "No"; and the consensus of commentators, who have examined and reexamined the question over the course of what has by now become more than a century, is that the Supreme Court's answer was wrong—morally wrong, politically wrong, legally wrong. The Court's mistake was tragic in every literal sense that that word can embody; and I say that it might seem strange that this later group of judges, Stephen Field and his brethren, no matter what their attachment to the ethic of free enterprise, should so quickly and so thoroughly have repressed what might have been the great lesson of their youth. Certainly it had marked the lives of them all, every one, even if the troubles that arose from the slavery issue could then be largely confined to the South, once the war itself was over, and providing that the former slaves also could largely be confined there. But now in 1896, less than forty years later, a Michigan Republican named Brown told Plessy directly—and indirectly and with some time lag he told also Plessy's seventy million fellow citizens, black, white, red, and yellow—that he was segregated not by the Constitution, not by the Supreme Court, but by Mother Nature. And Henry Brown spoke for six colleagues as well as for himself, in language that is as racist —and unlike many public speakers nowadays, I do not use the adjective "racist" loosely—as any ever uttered by a Supreme Court justice: "Legislation is powerless to eradicate racial instincts [so that if] . . . one race be inferior to the other socially, the constitution of the United States cannot put them upon the same plane." [11] The only dissenter was John Marshall Harlan, a Kentuckian who like Taney had been born in a manor staffed with slaves.[12] But Harlan had come a long ways from the "Know Nothing" days of his youth; and he had profited from both his own, and from the nation's experience. "Our constitution," said Harlan, "is color-blind, and neither knows nor tolerates classes among citizens. In respect of civil rights, all citizens are equal before the law. . . . The destinies of the two races, in this country, are indissolubly linked together, and the interests of both require that the common government of all shall not permit the seeds of race hate to be planted under the sanction of law. . . . In my opinion, the judgment this day rendered will, in time, prove to be quite as pernicious as the decision made by this tribunal in the *Dred Scott* Case." [13] Of course he was right, but it took fifty-eight years for the Supreme Court to muster a majority who agreed with his views strongly enough to disavow *Plessy,* in a decision that came only a year before Harlan's grandson and namesake took his place as a member of the Court.

Stephen Field turned eighty in the year that *Plessy* was decided, and he had become notoriously both cantankerous and senile before then. He—like so many of the old men who have preferred (and who still prefer) to cling to the office of Supreme Court justice long past the time when their physical, mental, and social senses alike have become impaired[14]—was a dubious person to be a political leader helping to shape the way of life of twentieth-century Americans. But he did achieve his personal goal of outlasting Chief Justice Taney—under whom he had, of course, served —in length of tenure.

From Field's compelled retirement—his own colleagues

finally had demanded that he step down—to the end of World War I and of the Wilson administration is a period of about a quarter of a century. This was a time during which both spokesmen and actors for reform, social and political and economic, became increasingly strident in their demands for change in the conservative kind of policies that we have just examined. We might well ask, therefore, what kind of response came forth from that Court, while the rest of the American polity was reacting to the Populists, the muckrakers, and then the Progressives of both parties, before the war closed in and substituted, for the reform of social and economic inequities, the repression of personal liberties?

Certainly the Supreme Court acquiesced less completely, and less quickly, in the reforms following the turn of the century, than did the presidency, the Congress, and most of the state legislatures. On the other hand, the Supreme Court was probably less conservative than most of the rest of the judiciary, federal and state, during this time.

The Court was perhaps least sympathetic to the organization of workingmen into labor unions, and to the increase in labor's share of industrial income. Attempts by both Congress and various states to encourage union organization of railroad employees, by outlawing antiunion pledges as a condition of individual employment, were vetoed. The Court rejected also the policy that railroads could be held subject to suit for damages by employee victims of industrial accidents on the job, although in this instance, when Congress promptly reenacted the statute but with narrower application, a Court which included four new justices—and which excluded the three most negative members of the five-man majority that controlled the initial decision on this issue—acquiesced. State legislation to regulate the hours of employment was upheld for minors and for women, but these were viewed as exceptions to the general rule until Brandeis and Clarke joined the Court; shortly thereafter, in 1917, the Court switched sides on this issue and approved a general policy of state control over the hours of labor, and also a national policy of the eight-hour day for railroad labor. But in the very next year a majority disapproved of national regulation of the conditions of employment for children who worked in factories that produced goods for sale in other than local (that is, intrastate) markets. It should be noted, however, that in all of the latter three instances, disagreement was so strong that a bare majority of five controlled, no matter which way the decision went. State systems of compulsory workmen's compensation insurance also were approved in 1917 but again by a minimal majority of five justices. Contrariwise, in the same year and by the same margin, the Court disapproved of state regulation of employment agencies.

During the early part of this period, the Interstate Commerce Commission was overruled by the Supreme Court in fifteen out of sixteen chances.[15] After 1906, however, the Court just as consistently approved the actions of the ICC, and confirmed its authority to establish both inter and intrastate railroad rates. On the other hand, several intrastate railroad rate structures, established by various states, were disapproved by the Court as too low and unfair to the railroad companies.

The trend in the Court's antitrust policies went in the opposite direction—from positive to negative. Teddy Roosevelt's trust-busting prosecutions of both Wall Street and the Chicago stockyards were upheld, and so (late in Taft's term in the White House) were prosecutions against Standard Oil and American Tobacco. Thereafter, however, the Court withdrew its support, finding that although national combinations in shoe manufacturing machinery and the United

States Steel Corporation might be monopolies, they were not "unreasonable" ones.

The Court did support the regulation, for public health and safety, of various consumer goods sold in the national market, by upholding the new food and drugs, meat inspection, and narcotics control statutes. Justified under the same rationale was a dairy farmers' bill to tax interstate sales of oleomargarine. An attempt to control international traffic in prostitutes was rejected by the Court, although it did approve a federal statute to regulate the interstate market for commercialized sex. Many of the major economic reforms of the first term of the Wilson administration (including the Federal Reserve System, the Federal Farm Land Banks, the Underwood Tariff, the Clayton Anti-trust Act, and the Federal Trade Commission) were not subjected to audit by the Court, during the early years of these programs. The relatively drastic wartime controls over food, housing, transportation, and much else in the economy, were of course given the Court's imprimatur. So also, as the period drew to a close, were some rather collectivistic ventures in public enterprise that a few states had authorized. Prohibition, initially as a national policy of support for local (state) option, subsequently as a wartime measure to conserve food, and then as a requirement of the newly adopted Eighteenth Amendment, was consistently upheld by the Supreme Court.

Decisions by the Court on questions of civil liberty were few and far between, during the first two decades of this century. There were two attempts to suggest the possibility that such components of fair procedure in state courts as the right to indictment by a grand jury, to trial by jury, and to be secure from testimonial compulsion, ought to be recognized by the Supreme Court as among the privileges and immunities of citizens of the United States, or as an aspect of that due process of personal liberty which states should not deny. Only Harlan agreed, dissenting alone as he had in the only previous similar case. On the other hand, the Court approved the invasion of personal privacy, that was necessary for the larger social interest in public health, by compulsory vaccination. And the Court also upheld—although, it should be noted, for a white-collar, businessman defendant—a policy that in *federal* courts evidence resulting from illegal searches would be inadmissible. The novel basis for this was asserted to be the Supreme Court's supervisory authority over lower federal courts. The Court also upheld an alien's claim to civic equality in the right to work, and it disapproved an attempt to zone residential housing explicitly for racial segregation. Once the war came along, however, the Court gave its full support (as it always had done in the past) to whatever repression of civil liberties the rest of the government deemed necessary to the successful conquest of the nation's enemies. Thus the Court upheld the draft and the suppression of pacifist and other political dissent, taking the position that to whatever extent patriotism might require, political freedom would be curtailed for the duration. In the language of the thrice-wounded Union veteran who spoke for the unanimous Court in one of these decisions, "When a nation is at war many things that might be said in time of peace are such a hindrance to its effort that their utterance will not be endured so long as men fight and that no Court could regard them as protected by any constitutional right." [16]

Taft's Team in the Twenties

The delayed effect of World War I was to increase considerably the volume of cases in the federal courts during the twenties, due in part to increased national regulation of both economic and personal behaviors. The major questions were considered to be economic ones stemming from both state and national legislative and administrative regulation of business and labor, from contracting and bankruptcy problems that were the by-products of the war, and from the recently adopted income tax amendment. Questions of fair procedure in criminal law enforcement were raised by the novel and considerably increased federal police activity consequent to the regulation of interstate and foreign commerce in narcotics, white slavery, smuggling, auto theft, and of course, by no means least, of prohibition, which was peculiarly the national social problem during this decade. Least attention continued to be given, by the Supreme Court, to issues of personal and political freedom, which at this time were identified primarily with the radical left— Bolsheviks, Trotskyites, and Wobblies—upon whom considerable publicity focused in the early years of the decade, as a consequence of the "red-busting" activities that had been initiated by Wilson's attorney general, although this diversion became shunted aside by the even more newsworthy looting of the national domain that soon began to preempt the attention of several members of the Harding cabinet.

Especially during the first half dozen years under Taft, until the Chief began to lose his control over the Court, it continued its reactionary policy of hostility toward labor unions, and toward social legislation intended to ameliorate the conditions of labor. In what at the time were considered to be leading decisions, the Court disapproved of peaceful picketing, vetoed for the second time a congressional plan to regulate child labor, rejected minimum wage controls for women and children, unanimously repudiated the un-American idea of compulsory labor arbitration, disapproved a labor boycott as a monopoly in restraint of interstate commerce, unanimously held another union liable in triple damages under the Sherman Anti-trust Act because it was

15

deemed guilty of a conspiracy to obstruct interstate commerce, and approved an injunction against a state minimum wage statute. Only occasionally were labor interests upheld, as in the denial of an employer's claim to recover property damages from a striking union, and in the Court's confirmation of its earlier approval of state regulation of the hours of work for female employees.

The Court was conservative, rather than reactionary, in its policies toward national or state regulation of business, rejecting only about half of the claims of governmental authority that it considered. This observation masks the fact that there were, however, important differences in the orientation of the Court toward national, as distinguished from state, economic regulation. Most of the Court's decisions concerned state regulation, which it tended to disallow, while at the same time it supported most instances of national regulation. Thus the Court upheld unanimously the policy of an integrated national system of transportation (stated in the Transportation Act of 1920), and the new policy of administrative rate making for the tariff, and by large majorities upheld both the regulation of stockyards and the federal reserve system of national banking control. But a complicated federal system of joint national-state regulation of grain futures markets was disapproved. The Court upheld some but rejected other state plans for taxing the property or the franchises of "foreign" (to use the quaint legalism for a business incorporated in some state other than the one levying the tax) corporations. It also upheld the principle of municipal zoning, and state plans for the control of reemployment rights, and for the removal of diseased trees (which were threatening the Byrd apple orchards; this was in Virginia) at private rather than public expense. Much more frequent, however, were Court rulings that states could not interfere with private enterprise, by attempting to do such things as to control railroad rates, or to regulate employment agencies, or the sale of steamship tickets for transoceanic voyages, or their own natural resources, or collectivize the control of cotton gins, or regulate chain stores, or control corporate access to state courts. All of the preceding decisions, it is true, drew dissents; but the Court unanimously rejected a policy proposal that would have limited education, for children between eight and sixteen years of age, to that provided by public enterprise.

The Court accepted the new federal Maternity Act of 1921, which distributed child welfare grants; but on the core humanitarian issue of fiscal claims by the relatively underprivileged—employees who suffered industrial accidents, passengers injured by railroads, homeowners whose cottages were excavated from below by coal mines—the United States Supreme Court stood pat. Many such claims were on the threshold of disappearing from the Court's docket anyhow, for reasons that I shall discuss in Chapter III; and the Court's typical function, in processing these characteristically common (that is, state) law cases, was to proffer an ultimate escape hatch that legitimized legal irresponsibility for corporate litigants that had lost out in the state courts below. Many *state* courts had developed by this time progressive policies to cover such matters as (to put it in the legal idiom) the maintenance of attractive nuisances (such as poisoned but clear and cool-appearing swimming pools) for the enticement of children on hot summer days.

The many prohibition enforcement cases provided an opportunity for the Court to explore for the first time some of the implications of a federal system of law enforcement— by which I mean one that involved interaction between several dozen administratively autonomous state and several thousand local police systems, both with each other and with the national police agencies, of which the most conspicuous, the FBI, emerged during this period, under the direction of the man who remained, after forty years, in the same role. With rare exceptions (including one that approved the use of the presidential pardon as a political instrument in what was then Al Capone's town; and another that disapproved having municipal politicos preside over criminal trials), the Court was creative in developing rules of judicial policy that supported convictions, at whatever sacrifice to the fairness of the procedures, or to the privacy of the defendants. Thus the same offense could be independently prosecuted by both the national and a state government; arbitrary searches and seizures of automobiles were not unreasonable; false arrest under illegal warrants did not invalidate a consequent conviction; and the government was free to use illegally wiretapped evidence, to support the conviction of a gang of Seattle smugglers and bootleggers.

The Court's attitude toward claims of right to fair procedure, for defendants other than bootleggers, was not markedly different. During the 1921 term, for example, the Court did declare unconstitutional a federal statute that permitted prosecution on information (rather than only after indictment by a grand jury) in the municipal courts of the District of Columbia, under the rationale that a juvenile court commitment to the workhouse, for nonsupport, was an "infamous crime"; but the other half dozen criminal defendants, whose cases were considered by the Court in this term, had their convictions affirmed. Similarly, a check of the 1925 term shows that the Court decided eight cases raising claims to fair procedure in criminal trials, all of which were decided unanimously, with two white-collar perjurers —one a bankrupt and the other a business executive who falsified his corporation's income tax returns—getting their convictions quashed on statute-of-limitations grounds, while the other half dozen—two embezzlers, a street brawler, a doctor who prescribed large doses of morphine to his long-time patient-addicts, a dope peddler, and two renegade-white murderers of a reservation Indian—all had their sentences approved. Claims to privacy, by persons other than bootleggers, fared no better. In a case decided the month that Taft joined the Court, but while the chief justiceship still remained vacant, the government's use of evidence, consisting of papers that had been stolen by in-dustrial espionage agents and turned over to the federal prosecutor "on a silver platter" (as such acquisitions sub-sequently came to be called), was approved; and dealing with the only claim to physiological privacy that appears to have been passed upon during the decade, the Court gave its blessing to eugenical sterilization, with none other than Mr. Justice Holmes, then himself eighty-six years of age and a Malthusian since his youth, propounding for the Supreme Court the dubiously liberal policy that "society can prevent those who are manifestly unfit from continuing their kind" because "the principle that sustains compulsory vaccination is broad enough to cover cutting the Fallopian tubes." Holmes concluded with the aphorism that "three generations of imbeciles are enough"—an assertion that might be thought to raise more questions than it settles.[17]

Claims to civic equality were dealt with just as harshly. An elderly female pacifist was denied naturalization because she refused to take an oath to "bear arms." And in the 1922 term alone, the Supreme Court produced no less than three racially discriminatory decisions, ruling that resident Japa-nese aliens could be denied the right to own property—the reference to "persons" in the Fourteenth Amendment, which purports now as then to forbid any state "to deny to any person within its jurisdiction the equal protection of the laws," was intended to refer to *un*natural persons like business corporations, but not to natural persons who were aliens. For the same reason, Japanese aliens could be precluded from becoming naturalized citizens of the United States. So too, incidentally, could Hindus, because when federal statutes referred to "white persons," the commonsensical everyday lay meaning was intended, and not some esoteric scientific classification such as "Caucasian." A few years later an American child of United States citizenship (but Chinese ancestry) was found to be "pure" Chinese rather than "pure" white—this was in 1927; by the next year it would not have been surprising for Taft to have substituted the more popular Republican adjective "lily"—and therefore bound to attend whatever high school facility, if any; the Supreme Court didn't know—the State of Mississippi might be providing for members of the colored race, like her. These last three decisions were all unanimous, having been acquiesced in by Brandeis and Holmes—and with regard to the Chinese-American child, by Stone too. But the Taft Court did manage to produce one relevant decision that was not racist: it disapproved a state statute explicitly denying to Negroes the right to participate in Democratic party primary elections in the State of Texas.

More claims to political freedom were heard by the Court in the twenties than in any previous decade, but most of them were rejected. Postal censorship was upheld; and the Court disapproved peaceful propagation of Communist dogma, affirming prosecutions under various older state statutes that proscribed such philosophical offenses as "criminal anarchism" and "criminal syndicalism." The appeals of two IWW organizers, from different states, came to opposite conclusions, the Court reversing the Kansas conviction for which the state had presented no evidence other than the cards that had been issued to joiners. But the Court unanimously upheld the conviction of a New York Ku Klux Klansman, prosecuted under the state's then recent and so-called "Civil Rights" law, for the offense of belonging to a secret society. The only strong stand in behalf of political freedom that the Court took in the entire decade came quite early, when it vetoed several midwestern state products of postwar hysteria (against the recent enemy) which had taken the form of legislation prohibiting either public or private school instruction in the German language. The Court's attitude toward personal liberty was well summed up in the majority opinion of a 1922 decision that was economically so relatively liberal that the then three most conservative members (McReynolds, Van Devanter, and Taft) dissented, although it is to be presumed that they, as well as the majority (which included Clarke and Holmes and Brandeis) accepted this particular *obiter dictum*: ". . . neither the Fourteenth Amendment nor any other provision of the Constitution of the United States imposes upon the states any restrictions about 'freedom of speech' or the 'liberty of silence'; nor, we may add, does it confer any right of privacy upon either persons or corporations." [18]

The issue that really exercised the Supreme Court, meas-ured in terms of either a quantitative or a qualitative stand-ard, was one that had nothing very much to do with either economic rights or civil liberties: whether the president could fire such partisan political appointees as postmasters, without the consent of the Senate. The quantitative stand-ard that I have applied in appraising the amount of im-portance that the Court itself attributed to this issue is a simple one: length of space allocated to the report of the case. During the twenties the Court was deciding on the merits around three hundred cases per term—about two-thirds again as many as would be true after World War II —but it was justifying these decisions with much briefer opinions than were to become common during the thirties. The average decision was allocated less than eight pages in the *United States Reports* during the twenties; but the *Myers* case of 1926, a claim for back salary in behalf of a by-then deceased ex-postmaster whom Wilson had both appointed and removed, was by far the longest of the decade and consumed two hundred and forty-four.

The qualitative standard I have applied is the amount of attention the decision attracted among the leading constitutional law scholars of the day: Howard Lee McBain had an article in print almost contemporaneously with the decision; Edward Corwin came out with an article and a pamphlet the following year; James Hart brought out a book a couple of years later; and there were various other articles in the law reviews. The author of the majority opinion followed unflinchingly the views that he had proffered in a precedent statement, in the form of a series of lectures (entitled *Our Chief Magistrate and His Powers*) during the interregnum between his terms as president, and as chief justice; and for some time I have been,[19] and I remain, of the opinion that what could (and what probably otherwise would) have been an obscure case with a summary affirmance was given not merely the full, but simply extraordinary treatment (with George Wharton Pepper appearing as amicus curiae for the United States Senate) because the chief justice happened to be an ex-president, who seized upon the opportunity— which might well not have arisen again during his lifetime —to manipulate constitutional rhetoric so as to justify his own unhappy role as president in the sordid Glavis-Ballinger affair of 1910.[20] Brandeis, who had argued Glavis's case then, remained in dissent. It was thus his own claim that Taft was passing upon; and he did his best to state a policy that would support a strong president in leading the country—a role that Taft himself never has been accused of having fulfilled.

To sum up, the Court during the twenties continued, and in several respects intensified, the reactionary labor and conservative business policies that had been developed during the earlier years of the century; it did give considerably more time and attention to claims of personal liberty and right, but tended to support very conservative policies for the disposition of these issues; and it chose as its cause célèbre an issue which, in the idiom of today's radical left in the political science profession, would most certainly be castigated as "pseudopolitical," one that was phony because it had little or nothing to do directly (or even, in any empirically demonstrable way, indirectly) with the social, economic, or even political interests of most Americans, in either Taft's day or our own.

The Nine Old Men

There has been an understandable tendency, in discussing the Supreme Court's political role during the thirties, to exaggerate the reactionary constitutional posture assumed by the Nine Old Men of the Hughes Court during the early and middle years of the decade. A dispassionate examination of the record discloses, however, that the immediate consequence of the substitution of Hughes and Roberts for Taft and Sanford was a pronounced shift to the left, particularly in regard to issues of civil liberties. It is necessary to recall, of course, that when the Court convened for the 1930 term, Hoover had been in office only a year and a half, the worst of the depression was yet to come, and it was to be over four years before any of the New Deal programs of emergency economic regulation was passed upon by the

THE CONSTITUTIONAL POLITY

Court. Most of the economic decisions upheld the government, including a federal antitrust prosecution, both ICC and state regulation of railroads, and state corporate franchise taxation. Both state regulation of insurance companies and state taxation of chain stories were upheld over the dissents of the four conservatives (Van Devanter, Sutherland, Butler, and McReynolds), although a state estate tax was invalidated in what is apparently one of the only three instances (the second occurring in the following year, and the third immediately *after* the so-called "switch in time," in May of 1937) in which Hughes voted to create a conservative majority, that is, when the Court otherwise was equally divided between the four conservatives, on the one hand, and Roberts and the three liberals, on the other. In other conservative decisions the Court disapproved orders of the ICC and FTC, an antitrust prosecution of dealer licensing by Standard Oil, and a state tax on interstate motor transport. The Court upheld the right to privacy by requiring the suppression of illegal evidence in a prohibition case, upheld fair procedure by reversing the conviction of an airplane thief (who had been prosecuted under the National Motor Vehicle Theft Act), and upheld claims to political freedom by a teen-age female Young Communist League member (who led salutes to a red flag at a summer youth camp), and by the publisher of a scurrilous weekly scandal sheet. The change that had taken place in the Court's orientation toward civil liberties is illustrated by contrasting, with the dictum quoted above from the first year of the Taft Court, the following statement by Chief Justice Hughes, speaking for a majority of himself plus Roberts and the three liberals in the latter decision, and over the dissents of the four conservatives: "It is no longer open to doubt that the liberty of the press and of speech is within the liberty safeguarded by the due process clause of the

Fourteenth Amendment from invasion by state action." [21] The marginality of the Court's policy position was equally demonstrated, however, by two decisions of the preceding week which went the opposite way, with Roberts then joining the four conservatives to persist in the Taft Court's policy of denying civic equality to female and other pacifists who refused, in exchange for naturalization, to promise to bear arms in any wars that might involve the nation.

Beginning with the 1931 term, however, Hughes and Roberts voted much more frequently with the four conservatives to disallow the very same type of economic regulation (viz., ICC rate orders, state taxes on business, state control over corporations) that the Court had tended to uphold during Hughes's and Roberts's first term. Moreover, there were an unusually large number of economic underdog cases, typically suits by injured rail-workers or passengers against the roads; and in the eight such cases that I noticed, not a single pro-claimant vote was registered by any member of the Court, not even in the case of the five-year-old trespasser who had not heeded the sign to stay off a trestle from which older boys were suffered to dive into a canal, even though two lower federal courts (who were, of course, reversed by the unanimous Hughes Court) had agreed that the child should be compensated for the leg which he had lost while playing on the Erie Railroad's attractive nuisance. There were very few civil liberties decisions, and they mostly concerned prohibition enforcement, although El Paso Negro dentist L. A. Nixon won the second round in his continuing legal battle to be allowed to participate in the Texas Democratic primary election.

Thereafter, for the next several terms, the Court continued to serve as self-appointed censor of governmental interference—federal or state—in what remained of the American system of free enterprise during the worst years of the Depression. I refer here to the ongoing, nonemergency actions of federal and state administrative agencies, such as tax collectors, and railroad and other utilities commissioners. Some were upheld as lawful in their activities, others were stigmatized as unconstitutional. The Court giveth, and the Court taketh away. Most of the few fair procedure and privacy claims heard were upheld, although what had been their principal source (prohibition enforcement) petered out after the middle of the 1933 term. The Court continued to define "white" on the basis of community standards of racial prejudice rather than in ethnological terms; and the claim that one might be deemed exempt from military training as a condition of university education at land-grant institutions was unanimously rebuffed. The first two decisions passing upon state emergency economic controls—New York milk marketing, and Minnesota mortgage moratorium plans—were upheld, but in both instances over the dissents of the four conservatives. The first New Deal decision was not announced until January of 1935, and it was foreboding: only Cardozo protested the Court's invocation of an ancient and irrelevant common law dogma—replete with a Latin maxim, *delegatus non potest delegare*—which meant that Roosevelt could not direct General Hugh "Ironpants" Johnson to administer an industry production code for the control of hot (that is, contrary to plan) oil shipments. The president was supposed to run the petroleum industry personally, because Congress had given *him* the "power" (whatever that could mean) to do so—although both the Court's policy, and the rhetoric with which the Court purported to justify it, were directly opposed to a century of national political experience, and to the Court's own precedent decisions, to say nothing of the requirements for running the government in a modern industrialized country even under nonemergency circumstances.[22] *Panama Refining Co.* was not just an economically conservative decision—such as was, for example, another announced the same day, in which the Court unanimously refused to uphold the ICC's policy that power reverse gears should be substituted for manually operated ones on railroad steam locomotives, with Brandeis justifying the outcome by pointing out that "at common law the carriers were 'free to determine how their boilers should be kept in proper condition for use without unnecessary danger'." Evidently, the Federal Boiler Inspection Law had not yet succeeded in changing the common law, in this respect. Now *that* is a conservative decision—a few individual trains might be wrecked, but not the entire railroad industry. The Hot Oil decision, however, was reactionary. Instead of preserving the status quo, it represented an attempt to go back to a simpler way of national economic life, the one that had been Stephen Field's ideal. Moreover, it was somewhat less than candid. Soon the president was to be accused of deception, because he was to attack the Supreme Court for being too old when his real complaint was that it was too conservative; similarly, in this decision the Court's real objection was to the substance of the detailed regulation of production, industry practices, and the conditions of labor contained in the National Recovery Act codes. But the rhetoric of both Hughes's majority opinion and Cardozo's dissent is limited to the shadow issue of whether Franklin Roosevelt should—and neither Hughes nor Cardozo bothered to discuss the more important, and one would think logically prior question of "could"—administer the government in the manner of George Washington.[23] Of course, the Court's rationale was not without point, because if no president could run the national government, in 1935, in the manner suitable to its operations when the capital was located in New York, then many programs, including probably all of the emergency regulatory programs, could not be carried into effect. But it was, I submit, every bit as devious and dissimulative as was the rejoinder from the president, which was to follow two years later. And it was only the beginning.

It is true that the Court did continue to uphold some governmental economic regulation, both national and state, and both normal and emergency. The New Deal money controls, giving the Treasury a monopoly of the nation's gold supply; a New Jersey chain store tax; an Indiana statute regulating insurance companies; all were upheld over the dissents of the four conservatives, and so also would have been an ICC reparation order if Cardozo had not voted the wrong way. The decision approving the abrogation of clauses in both public and private contracts, for repayment in gold, was so obnoxious to McReynolds, at once the most irascible and conservative member of the Court, that he departed from the prepared text of his dissenting opinion, blurting out that "the Constitution . . . is gone." Clearly, there was a close identity between the Constitution and the gold standard in the eyes of this veteran of earlier political wars against Populist William Jennings Bryan. On civil liberties questions, the Court reversed the death sentences, after retrials, of the Scottsboro defendants, and on the new ground of racial discrimination in the selection of the convicting juries; but the Court was also unanimous in its agreement that Texas finally had discovered a legally acceptable basis upon which to continue to exclude Negroes from participating in its Democratic party primary elections. And only the three liberals would even vote to hear a freedom of speech claim by a Communist organizer who had been sentenced to a Georgia chain gang for his proselyting activities.

It was in the last week of May in 1935 that the Supreme Court clearly embarked upon a course designed to repudiate the New Deal and bring the nation back to its senses.

Unanimously, the Court declared unconstitutional the National Industrial Recovery Act, the national emergency farm bankruptcy act, and the president's attempt to control through replacement of the chairman, the regulatory policies of the Federal Trade Commission. (The first of these decisions typically is denigrated, in constitutional law discussions that wittingly or not purport to trivialize the NRA program by so doing, as the "sick chicken" case, evidently by scholars born sufficiently affluent to have been spared the necessity of having their families' meat purchased in ghetto butcher shops where the possibility of ptomaine poisoning is no joke.) Three weeks earlier the three liberals and Hughes had protested the invalidation of the national Railroad Retirement Act, losing the decision because Roberts went with the conservatives, who did not deny that the railroads were engaged in interstate commerce; instead, they fell back upon the undefined and boundless reservoir of judicial policy discretion that is subsumed under the concept of substantive due process—and the latter characterization applies irrespective whether the constitutional peg be the Fifth or the Fourteenth Amendment, and irrespective whether the substance be property or personal rights.

The 1935 term was distinguished primarily by two things. First, there was an intensification of the ideological gulf between the three liberals and the four conservatives; and second, there was a shift in the focus of major federal policy issues that were considered, away from the temporary programs of emergency administration and toward the key components in what was intended to be an expanded and continuing program of economic reform. Thus the Agricultural Adjustment Act and the Securities Act (both of 1933) were the first to incur the Court's disapproval, gaining support only from the three liberals; both the labor and the price-fixing sections of the Bituminous Coal Conservation

Act of 1935, and the Municipal Bankruptcy Act of 1934,
were disapproved when Hughes, but not Roberts, joined the
liberals; and only the TVA received the Court's imprimatur,
with McReynolds dissenting alone. Part of the New York
milk-marketing system was upheld, and part of it was rejected, the óutcome in each case depending strictly upon
which way Hughes and Roberts voted. But in many ways
perhaps the boldest—and certainly the most reactionary—
decision of the term was the one in which Roberts joined
the four conservatives to veto the New York minimum wage
plan for women employees, in a case that was almost a mirror
image of one thirteen years earlier, with the same four
conservative justices plus one moderate forming a majority
of five to define a national judicial policy of hostility to
minimum wage regulations even for women, and with the
chief justice and the liberals in dissent.[24] *Adkins* clearly
had been a conservative failure to follow the liberal precedents that the Court had established in 1908, and again in
1917, when it had approved policies of wages and hours
regulation for women; and the 1936 rejection of that same
policy can only be described, I repeat, as reactionary. Roberts
left a self-serving memorandum in which he purported to
explain his vote; but even if one were prepared to accept
his own explanation for his behavior, the result is the more
poignant, because his statement indicates a total failure to
appreciate what would be the implications of his choice, not
only for the country but for the Court as well.[25] Otherwise,
the Court was preoccupied with the usual grist for its mill,
but with the difference that in this term even the ordinary
federal and state economic controls were almost entirely
rejected. Thus a state corporation tax, several applications
of the federal income tax to capital gains, a federal excise
tax, state income tax, state property tax applied to a railroad, and state gasoline storage tax, all were upheld only by

the three liberals, who were joined by the chief justice in dissenting against the majority's refusal to support the commissioner in two applications of the federal estate tax. The Court upheld the collection of the federal estate tax in a third case, in which the conservatives lost the support of Roberts. Civil liberties were substantially ignored during the 1935 term, although the Court did purport to uphold the freedom of the press, by declaring invalid Huey Long's state excise tax on the New Orleans and Baton Rouge newspaper industry; and it did initiate the judicial policy that states could not legally compel defendants to incriminate themselves.

Stone was quite ill and unable to participate during the first half of the 1936 term, and the Court's output was routine: half a dozen state tax and regulatory decisions, mostly adverse, were announced, and one unanimous decision supported the political freedom of a Communist organizer in Oregon. It is notable that during these five months while Stone was absent, it was impossible for the four conservatives to lose any decision that they opposed, because the remaining justices were too few to form a majority (and any even divisions would be held over to await Stone's return). Stone did return on February 1, and four days later the president delivered his message, to the Congress and to the country, proposing that the Supreme Court be reorganized to make it more efficient.

The efficiency of the Court, in the sense in which the president was interested, began to improve at once. As Pritchett has reported,[26] thirteen of the decisions from then to the end of the term were 5–4 divisions; and of these, twelve were ones in which the four conservatives were forced into dissent, because *both* Hughes and Roberts voted with the three liberals, instead of disagreeing (as they had done as recently as February 1, and as they frequently had done in previous terms) or instead of voting with the four conservatives (as they had done most of the time in the term immediately preceding). These dozen marginal but liberal decisions upheld again the gold clause abrogation; state milk-marketing price regulations; a state minimum wage law for women (and expressly overruled the *Adkins* precedent, while confining *Tipaldo* to its own special facts); upheld in a series of cases the National Labor Relations Act, and the policy of federal regulation of labor-management relations in the basic industries, even (and notwithstanding the tender solicitude for freedom of the press, articulated by the four conservatives in dissent) as applied to newspapers; upheld a state labor relations act, and a state unemployment compensation tax; and—most wonderful of all to behold—even upheld in two cases the Social Security Act of 1935, with its evolutionary implications for putting a floor under the poverty level for at least some of the more disadvantaged classes of society. Moreover, by an equivalent 4–3 division (with Stone and Van Devanter paired in non-participation) the Court upheld a state tax on chain stores. Larger majorities upheld the New York State income tax; federal regulation of shipping; the Wisconsin state use tax; an ICC regulation; and the collection of agricultural processing taxes reenacted in 1936 after the Court's decision earlier that year invalidating the Agricultural Adjustment Act. Unanimous decisions upheld the federal Railway Labor Act; the national farm bankruptcy act enacted to replace the one that the Court had rejected two years earlier; the National Firearms Act; a state public health law; and a state tax on natural gas pipeline companies.

During this same three-month period economically conservative decisions were few. The Court unanimously disapproved a California tax on used car dealers, a railroad worker's Federal Safety Appliance Act claim, and an Ohio telephone rate schedule. The Court also disagreed with an ICC order that had the effect of requiring the Seaboard Air Line Railroad to extend its line to include the Fort Benning military base, and it upheld two affluent taxpayers in their dispute with the federal commissioner of internal revenue over depletion allowances for Texas oil wells. There was also one decision in which the chief justice voted inconsistently with his usual position: in a case where Roberts agreed with the three liberals, Hughes voted with the four conservatives to reject a Georgia statute regulating insurance companies. So the switch in time, that saved Nine, was not quite without its error variance. But it certainly was evidence of a sharp, clear, and abrupt change in the direction of the socioeconomic policies supported by the Supreme Court. As for who switched, individually, there can be no question whatsoever about that: mostly Roberts changed, and to a lesser extent, Hughes. And for the past thirty years and more, it has been a change from which there has been no turning back.

But the recounting of the 1936 term is not complete without notice of the Court's civil liberty policy. Two fair procedure claims were upheld, and three rejected, all unanimously; the most notable decision came in the 5–4 reversal of the conviction of the same Communist party organizer whose free speech claim the Court had refused even to consider two years earlier. The difference between the present and the earlier decision, in the case of Angelo Herndon, was the same as the difference in the outcome of the New Deal legislation that the Court upheld during the spring of 1937: Hughes and Roberts had voted with the four conservatives in the 3–6 decision in *Herndon v. Georgia*,[27] while in *Herndon v. Lowry*[28] they voted with the three liberals. And even more than the better publicized decisions of that time in which the Supreme Court acquiesced in the New Deal's social and economic changes, the path to the future, pointing the direction in which increasingly the Court's policy making would be developed, was signified by the reversal in Herndon's case.

The events of that winter and spring were a turning point of the very first magnitude in the redefinition of the Supreme Court's role in the American constitutional polity. Before 1937, the Court in this century devoted by far most of its time and attention to providing a sympathetic forum for a variety of minority economic and social interests which, having lost political battles in the legislative and executive arenas of the national and state and local governments, frequently gained a reprieve, and often a total exemption, from the Court. Since 1937, the Court has given up in substantial measure the role of inhibiting economic egalitarianism, and it has ceased to interfere with the exercise of legislative and administrative initiative in policy making in that respect. Instead, the Court increasingly has assumed a role of national leadership in the establishment of policies of social and political egalitarianism, providing a forum in which conflicting minority social and economic interests have pressed their claims to induce the Court to produce favorable norms and an appropriate supporting rhetoric, which these same interests can then use in other arenas of the American political system, as a lever to press for extensions of their judicial victories.

Economic Policy Since 1937

The "hard fact of life," as Arthur Selwyn Miller has put it, is the "desuetude of the Supreme Court in economic matters." [29] The Court since 1936 has relied exclusively upon what it can do through statutory interpretation as the boundary to the limits of its own competence in national economic policy making. By this I explicitly mean that the Court has used constitutional interpretation only in the supportive sense of expanding the recognized scope of legitimacy of congressional authority, in relation to the states, in relation to the presidency, and in relation to administrative agencies—but *not*, of course, in relation to civil liberties claims—and the Court has in both theory and practice renounced as an instrument of judicial policy making adverse judicial review of congressional economic and social legislation.[30] The Court continues, however, to participate in the development of many sectors of national economic policy: antitrust is a conspicuous example of continuing involvement by the federal judiciary in cooperation with the Department of Justice, the Federal Trade Commission, and committees of both houses of the Congress, all of which share with the Supreme Court a feudal sort of power of supervision, over both the lower courts and the administrative agencies.[31] Bankruptcy administration is even more conspicuously a field in which the federal district courts, subject to the primary supervision of the federal courts of appeals, and the more general policy control of the Supreme Court and of committees of the Congress, develop national economic policy. A third is the field of legalized monopolies, in regard to which Martin Shapiro has pointed out how

> in the patent field the Supreme Court's announcement in 1966 that the standard of invention is a constitutional rather than purely a statutory one has some tactical significance in strengthening the Court's hand. But by that time the judiciary had been intervening in Patent Office decisions for over a hundred years without it having been decided whether their review was constitutional or statutory. The decision that it was one and not the other does not promise to bring about any striking change in the tempo or substance of judicial intervention. In short, patent officials, inventors, patent lawyers,

and judges were able to negotiate and indeed battle
with one another intimately and sometimes furiously for
all those years without knowing the answer to the
seemingly essential preliminary question of whether they
were fighting over the Constitution or a patent statute,
and they will go on acting in roughly the same way now
that the earth-shaking question has been answered. Indeed they would have gone on in essentially the same
way if the question had been answered in just the opposite way or not at all. . . . Justice Douglas had for
years been campaigning to get the Court to declare its
functions in this field constitutional. In effect the Court
is staking out a position of political strength from which
to negotiate in future conflicts with the Patent Office.
. . . Incidentally . . . this episode neatly illustrates the
artificiality of dividing the constitutional from the non-
constitutional aspects of the Supreme Court's work . . .
[a]ny aspect of [which] is worthy or unworthy of special
attention not because it is constitutional or nonconstitu-
tional but because it has an important impact on public
policy or does not.[32]

Shapiro states a point of view that I have long shared;[33]
but it is nevertheless correct to point out that when the
Court chooses to work within the parameters of what purports to be congressional intent (or its analogues, executive
discretion, and administrative experience and expertise),
there is usually somewhat less room for the Court to pursue
a policy line in contradiction to, or even in independence
from, that of Congress, the presidency, and the administration.

The shift from constitutional to statutory criteria, for
judicial definition of the limits of governmental activity, has
been accompanied by the almost total disappearance of discussion about what Congress (or the national government)
can *do* (other than for occasional purposes of symbolic reinforcement, as the Supreme Court gives its blessing to what-

ever Congress happens to have done) *except* when congressional policy is questioned as impinging upon claims to personal liberty. Instead, claims in behalf of property right and economic interest have had to focus their queries, before the Supreme Court, upon whether administrators and lower courts are following the substance of congressional economic policy (properly understood); whether administrative or judicial or—to a much more limited extent—legislative procedures of decision making comport with the due process criteria that have been jointly formulated by Congress and the Supreme Court; and whether states have sought to extend their own economic policy making in such a way as to bring them into conflict with either action by the national government, or with each other.

According to data that Pritchett has reported, the Roosevelt Court's rate of support of federal administrative agencies ranged from a low of 60 per cent, for the Federal Trade Commission, to a high of 86 per cent, for the National Labor Relations Board. The only conspicuous exception was the Federal Communications Commission, which the Court upheld in only three of the eight decisions that Pritchett counted, for a rate of only 38 per cent; even so, the overall rate of average support was 72 per cent.[34] Tanenhaus found that, for the following decade (the 1947–1956 terms), the Court's overall rate of average support of federal administrative agencies was 69 per cent;[35] and Spaeth, in a partially overlapping study of the 1953–65 terms of the Warren Court found the virtually identical rate of 68 per cent for the first half (through the 1959 term)[36] and 78 per cent during the second half (the more recent period).[37] In the 1967 term, 84 per cent of the decisions that focused primarily upon judicial review of agencies favored them. Shapiro has remarked that although about a fifth of the Court's formal decisions now are concerned with the review of administrative agency determinations, there are "thousands of instances in which the circuit courts simply approve the agency position completely and the Supreme Court refuses certiorari, and . . . hundreds more in which the Court accepts certiorari and then totally supports the agency view." [38] His statement suggests that an alternative perspective from which to view the matter is that of how much agency decision making gets changed, as a sample of that which is produced. A standard work on administrative law points out that, during its first decade through the end of World War II, the Securities and Exchange Commission promulgated two thousand formal orders, of which only 5 per cent were judicially challenged, and only *three* orders—evidently, an average of one and one-half cases per thousand, or stated otherwise, one order every three years or so—were ultimately decided in whole or in part against the SEC;[39] and even at that one of these three was a pre-1937 decision of the Hughes Court.[40] If we turn to a different type of decision by the same agency, during roughly the same period of time over 6500 registration statements were filed, of which over three-fourths became effective (most of the others being withdrawn by the registrants as a consequence of informal negotiations between them and the commission's staff). Of the 182 instances in which the commission challenged the registrants by filing formal stop orders, only three were judicially reviewed, and in none of these did the lower court disagree with the agency.[41] It is in relation to this kind of hierarchical structure—almost solidly confirming and reinforcing the administrative agency in whatever economic policy goals it may be pursuing—that the rare issue that gets to the Supreme Court should be evaluated.

Martin Shapiro has explained the "relatively broad post-New Deal consensus" of the past quarter-century or so (and

he speaks primarily in relation to economic policy issues)
on the basis that judges and administrators have "quite
similar policy views" and equally tend to approve the statutory policies they jointly have been called upon to interpret.[42]
I have no doubt of the substantial correctness of Shapiro's
generalization, but it overemphasizes the homogeneity of
point of view between the Supreme Court and the remainder
of the administrative-adjudicatory bureaucracy. We have
indeed come a long way from the days of the Nine Old Men,
when Supreme Court justices were much more conservative
than federal administrators generally, and more so certainly
than many state administrators and lower court judges, both
state and federal. During most of the time since 1937,
however, and especially during the sixties, the Supreme
Court has been the most consistently liberal, as well as the
most liberal in an absolute sense, of any major policy-making
institution in the American polity. But it is not enough to
assume that the Supreme Court, by upholding administrative
decisions eight or nine times out of ten, necessarily is supporting liberal economic policies. In order to be more confident about that, it is necessary to ascertain whether the
Court approves the decisions of federal and state administrators, irrespective whether the decisions being reviewed
are economically liberal or conservative. If the Supreme
Court is indeed more liberal than the agencies, and if state
agencies tend to be more conservative than federal ones,
then we ought to expect that the Supreme Court will
approve a higher proportion of federal than of state administrative decisions; and that for either of these groups of
administrators, the Court will have tended to affirm economically *liberal* administrative decisions, and to *reverse*
conservative ones. I shall also distinguish between decisions
concerned with regulating business practices and competi-

tion, and those relating to labor unions, because this is a distinction that has seemed important to many Supreme Court justices during the past three decades.[43]

Pritchett's data for the Roosevelt Court,[44] that of Tanenhaus for the Vinson Court,[45] and Spaeth's for the Warren Court,[46] are not strictly equivalent, primarily because Pritchett's include only *split* decisions of the Supreme Court, and Tanenhaus's are restricted to *federal* agency regulation, while Spaeth's include both split and unanimous decisions of the Court and extend to both federal and state administrative regulation. To the extent that these studies are not comparable, we must, of course, temper with caution the findings of our comparison; but I believe that they are close enough to support the broad generalizations concerning policy trends that are our present concern. In regard to business regulation, the Supreme Court's rates of approval have been, by periods—Roosevelt: 58 per cent; Vinson: 61 per cent; Warren (1950s): 70 per cent; and Warren (early 1960s): 76 per cent. The equivalent ratios, for union support, are—Roosevelt: 68 per cent; Vinson: 55 per cent; Warren (1950s): 63 per cent; and Warren (early 1960s): 84 per cent. Evidently, the Court showed substantially more liberalism, in regard to both business regulation and labor support, during the Warren Court than in the earlier periods, particularly during the part (1960–1965) discussed by Spaeth, of the later period of the Warren Court. Support for unions fell off most noticeably during the Vinson Court period, and it was then when the Court made its most aggressively activist move into the arena of national economic (and indeed, indirectly but nevertheless by implication, military also) policy, when it invoked the rhetoric of the Constitution to chastize lame-duck Harry Truman for his symbolic seizure of several major steel mills, to avoid a strike in the midst of the Korean War.[47] I must emphasize that the Court freely acknowledged the power of Congress to have authorized the seizure, but existing statutes were interpreted not to authorize such a severe "deprivation" of the mill owners; and in opinions reminiscent of many of the 1935 term, a majority declared the president to have acted unconstitutionally. Because the effect of the seizure was interpreted to be, among other things, prounion, one interpretation that can be given to the Court's decision is that it was, certainly in part, antiunion in effect. Evidently, it could not have come at any other time than when it did, during the Vinson period and with an outgoing presidency at the nadir of its authority.

Pritchett's data show no important difference between the Roosevelt Court's 59 per cent rate of approval for federal business regulation, and 55 per cent rate for state regulation.[48] Spaeth's data for the first seven terms of the Warren Court (1953–60), with a federal approval rate of 70 per cent and a state rate of 61 per cent,[49] are consistent with the inference that the Warren Court gave even stronger support to governmental regulation of business than did the Roosevelt Court, and also that the relatively greater liberalism of federal, than of state, administrative agencies had increased during the fifties compared with the World War II period. Pritchett's data do not reveal the Roosevelt Court's approval rate for state labor cases, but his discussion, plus the detail that he does present, make it clear that the Court's approval rate of 71 per cent for the combined decisions of the National Labor Relations Board and the Fair Labor Standards Administrator, both of which were strongly supportive of organized labor during this period, was higher than the approval that the Court gave to the relatively few but generally antiunion state labor laws that it considered.[50] Spaeth's findings, for the early years of the Warren Court, certainly are consistent with such a reading of Pritchett.

Spaeth reports an approval rate of 66 per cent for federal regulation of labor cases, and of only 33 per cent for state cases. Part of this discrepancy is explained, however, by the fact that all of the state regulation was antiunion, whereas a majority of the federal cases were of prounion regulations; and as we shall see presently, the Court was also much more sympathetic to the federal prounion, than it was to the federal antiunion, regulatory decisions—although even the latter rate of 47 per cent approval was substantially higher than the 33 per cent rate of state approval.[51]

We can examine the relative liberalism of the Supreme Court, and of administrative agencies, by dividing each sample of agency decisions into those that were antibusiness (that is, liberal) and those that were probusiness. For Tanenhaus's sample, the Vinson Court agreed with 71 per cent of the liberal agency decisions, but agreed with only 33 per cent of the conservative (that is, probusiness) agency decisions.[52] Spaeth reports that the comparable ratios for the early period of the Warren Court were 78 per cent and 43 per cent, respectively.[53] If we ask the same question of the labor decisions (remembering that prounion is liberal, and antiunion conservative), the Vinson Court ratios are 69 per cent approval of prounion agency decisions, but only 15 per cent for antiunion agency decisions;[54] and for the Warren Court, 82 per cent approval of pro- and 47 per cent approval of anti-.[55] A further breakdown of Spaeth's data (89 per cent of unanimous, 74 per cent of split, for agency prounion; and 60 per cent of unanimous, 40 per cent of split, for agency antiunion) shows that the Warren Court tended to be more supportive of agencies in unanimous than in split labor decisions, irrespective whether the administrative decisions were pro- or antiunion. Note, however, that the range between approval ratios, 29 per cent for pro over con in unanimous Court decisions, and 34 per cent in split decisions, remains about the same, and that dividing the sample on the basis of Supreme Court dissensus does not change at all the finding that in the antibusiness and the prounion subsets of economic policy alike, both the Vinson and Warren Courts tended to support economically liberal administrative decisions, and to reverse conservative agency decisions. In short, the Supreme Court gave its support, most of the time, to the decisions of federal administrative agencies because those agencies, themselves, had made economically liberal decisions in most of their cases that reached the Supreme Court; and to the extent that the agencies made conservative decisions, the Supreme Court tended to disagree with them and to correct their policy errors.

There is one conspicuous, indeed, notoriously deviant case. Long before any of the studies by Pritchett and his successors, many observers had pointed out how completely the oldest of the federal regulatory agencies, the Interstate Commerce Commission, reflected in its supposed regulation of the railroad industry the interests primarily of the major railroads. Of course, the point has been generalized in the studies of an earlier generation of political scientists, to apply almost universally among both federal and state (to say nothing of municipal) agencies, regulatory and service alike. Nevertheless, the Supreme Court appears to have perceived a consistent relative difference in the conservatism of the ICC, in comparison with other federal regulatory agencies. Pritchett pointed out that the most liberal justices, who gave the highest support to all agencies except the ICC, were least supportive of it; while the conservative justices who were least sympathetic to the other agencies voted much more frequently, than did the liberals on the Court, to uphold the ICC;[56] and Spaeth has shown that the same distinction must be made for the Warren Court during the fifties,[57] a finding which I myself confirmed for the last four terms of the period Spaeth examined.[58] During that period, the Supreme Court affirmed and also decided in the economically liberal direction 75 per cent of the other-than-ICC federal regulatory agency cases: this was the same proportion as the agencies themselves had decided liberally. The ICC, however, had decided liberally only 14 per cent of its cases that the Supreme Court reviewed; and the Court reversed almost half of the ICC decisions in order to transform the ratio of liberal outcomes to 57 per cent.[59] My own data showed that the Supreme Court was just as liberal as the other federal regulatory agencies, and considerably more so than the ICC; and that the ten justices who served during the period were divided into two groups, of which every member of the first group (including Douglas, Black, Warren, Brennan, and Clark) voted less frequently in support of ICC decisions, and more frequently in support of the decisions of other federal regulatory agencies, than did any of the remaining members of the Court (Stewart, Burton, Harlan, Frankfurter, and Whittaker).

It has become not uncommon for the Court to push, actively, for more liberal economic policies on the part of all of its major clienteles, including not only the federal agencies but also Congress, lower federal courts, and state judges as well. For example, with only Frankfurter dissenting, the Court in 1946 directed the Federal Power Commission to go ahead and develop the agency's own policy under the Federal Power Act without deferring to lower courts for their interpretation of state statutes.[60] Two years earlier the Roosevelt Court had discarded several of its older and more conservative precedents to announce that, contrary to existing practices and the interpretation of the Constitution up to that time, the business of insurance was "in" interstate commerce and therefore subject to congressional regulation

—an invitation that the Congress quickly was to decline. A good illustration of the Court's policy guidance to lower courts is found in its manipulation of both its jurisdictional and substantive decisions, allocating a substantial part of its time to the reconsideration of the fiscal claims of economic underdogs (injured railway workers and seamen) in disputes that admittedly present no question of law, for the purpose of inducing both state and federal trial courts to acquiesce in proemployee jury verdicts,[61] thereby to some limited extent liberalizing a statute that had been as progressive as the Supreme Court would permit sixty years ago, but which now had become a conservative anachronism in comparison with the modern systems of workmen's compensation common in the states.

The Court has been not quite, but almost, as supportive of state as it has of federal economic policy making; and, just as we found to be true of the Court's review of federal agency decisions, Supreme Court justices tend to approve state policies that are prolabor and antibusiness, and to disapprove conservative state policies.[62] The Court no longer speaks of substantive due process as a limitation upon state economic regulation; and it is apparent that equal protection has almost disappeared from use. Arthur Miller states that with the possible exception of the previously mentioned Steel Seizure decision of 1952, "since 1937, the Court has invalidated only one minor state action that regulated the economy," that being an Illinois statute that exempted only American Express Company money orders from state regulation that included a licensing requirement.[63] The Court has also upheld a homeowner's property claim against a municipality for jet noise under an airport flight space, as a form of taking for which just compensation is guaranteed by the Fourteenth Amendment; here the Court did not use the phrase "substantive due process," although it is quite clear that that is the constitutional peg upon which the Court purported to rely.[64] In the same year, the Court upheld another homeowner's eminent domain claim against a municipality, although this time clearly on grounds of *procedural* due process.[65] Otherwise, the Supreme Court's invalidation of state economic controls, including state taxation, appears to have been confined either to conflicts that were conceptualized as relating to interstate commerce, or else to other explicit conflict between state and federal statutes such as a recent attempt to subject Red Cross employees to the Colorado unemployment compensation tax, which the Court disapproved on the ground that the American National Red Cross is a federal instrumentality subject to the exclusive regulation of congressional statutes, with which the state tax in this case was in conflict.[66] There have been at least a couple of dozen instances in which the Court has, since 1937, invalidated state legislation on commerce clause grounds, of which half occurred under the Roosevelt Court.[67] There have been a few decisions, mostly by the Roosevelt Court,[68] in which regulations concerning business or labor practices, state sales or use taxes, or state corporate income taxes have been disapproved by the Court, because (in the language of the formula that has been conventional since the days of John Marshall) they "burden commerce between the states"—that is, they interfere with free competition, and the norm of laissez faire, laissez passer. Probably the best known example of such a decision came in 1945, when the Roosevelt Court disapproved rail labor featherbedding in the guise of the Arizona Train Limit Law (of 1912!), which became a nuisance to transcontinental train operations with the outbreak of World War II.[69] More recently, the Warren Court has declared two state statutes taxing liquor sales, such as the New York attempt to cash in on sales to transoceanic passengers at Idlewild International Airport, to be an unconstitutional burden upon *foreign* commerce.[70] The Court's more usual rationale, however, in declaring invalid state attempts to regulate interstate commerce, has been that Congress has preempted the subject of the state regulation, and the resulting conflict must be resolved in favor of the national policy because of the Supremacy Clause. There were several such decisions during the forties, and again during the early sixties by the Warren Court.

As Spaeth has described the past decade and a half, "the Warren Court's decisions have been characterized by a strong attachment to the principles of economic liberalism: they have been prounion, antibusiness, procompetition, proemployee in personal-injury suits against employers, and prosmall business in a conflict between large and small business not involving antitrust action." [71]

The preceding discussion supports the following generalizations. First, only in regard to state regulation of industrial relations that affect interstate or foreign commerce has the Supreme Court continued to veto, in any important way, the economic policies of the various states. Second, much of even that limited veto has occurred only in the context of the Court's support for a counterpart congressional policy of economic control; and the ordinary effect of the Court's veto of state economic regulation has been to liberalize what had been the state policy. Third, the Court has not openly disapproved congressional economic policy, although the Court can and has (through the guise of statutory interpretation) undercut statutory economic policies in many discrete policy sectors. Fourth, when the Court has interpreted new policies into statutes, it has been almost invariably because the Court has sought to establish a more liberal economic policy than Congress has enacted. Fifth, the Court has shared in the development (usually euphemistically called the "administration") of many statutory policies with federal administrative agencies, and most of the time the Court has approved administrative policy. Sixth, when the Court has disapproved federal administrative policy, it has usually been to make it more economically liberal.

Civil Liberties Since 1937

The major change that has occurred since 1937 is that the Supreme Court gradually has become *more* liberal in its policy orientation than either Congress or any of the state legislatures. Instead of a conservative court vetoing the liberal innovations of Congress, the political dilemma of the past generation has been that of a conservative Congress that either has followed haltingly and reluctantly, or else has attempted to curb, the liberal policy innovations of the Supreme Court. Particularly under Warren, the Court has been transformed into a decision-making group that frequently provides an active, creative response to interests that have failed to gain support from Congress or the administration. Not a single act of Congress was declared unconstitutional on economic grounds from May 25, 1936 until April 21, 1969, when a District of Columbia residency requirement for welfare assistance was, together with two similar state statutory provisions, declared by the Court to deny equal protection to impoverished migrants (*Washington* v. *Legrant,* 394 U.S. 618 [1969]); and this was of course a pro-economic underdog—and therefore an economically libertarian—decision. Otherwise without exception, the invalidations since 1936 have been exclusively on civil libertarian grounds and, under the Warren Court, those of the elimination of congressional barriers to civic and political equality, or else of fair procedure. Similarly, the Court's invalidation of state legislation has been limited almost entirely to instances where more conservative state policies have conflicted with more liberal national ones, or where the Court has sought to eliminate state barriers to the nationalization, on a more liberal basis equivalent to the goals that the Court has postulated for the federal government, of civil rights and liberties.

This shift in the Court's policy goals and emphases has meant that cases raising economic issues no longer dominate the Court's dockets, as they clearly did before the Roosevelt Court. Even during the 1941–46 terms the ratio was seven economic to three civil liberties decisions; and thereafter the Court tended, from the end of World War II until about six years ago, to give equal emphasis to questions of civil liberties and to those of economic policy.[72] Beginning with the 1963 term, however, the average proportions have been 56 per cent for civil liberties, and 28 per cent for economic issues for the last six terms, a reversed ratio of 2 to 1 in favor of civil liberties over economic questions. The change, from 2 per cent civil liberties decisions (6/308) in Taft's first term (1921) to over 60 per cent half a century later in what was Warren's last term, evidently is best understood as a gradual but accelerating increase in civil liberties cases, beginning during World War I and continuing to increase at a modest rate through the end of World War II, followed by a steady increase until the early sixties when an even more rapid rise began. The Court established in 1945 a second (the Miscellaneous) docket, which for the past twenty-odd years has not consisted of "miscellaneous" cases at all— that is the function of the other (the Appellate) docket— but rather contains almost exclusively certiorari petitions *in forma pauperis*—that is, claims to fair procedure and to the right to privacy by state, and also by federal, criminal defendants. These miscellaneous certs by now consist of well over half of all cases docketed, and they are the source of the largest number of cases now being decided, for any of the categories discussed here.

During the Vinson Court and Warren's initial two terms, the average proportion of economic and civil liberties issues decided by the Court, to the total of decisions on the merits, was 58 per cent. For the subsequent period of the 1955 through the 1968 terms, the proportion was 81 per cent; and the increase has been due almost entirely to the increase in civil liberties decisions—and especially during the sixties. Moreover, there was a corresponding increase in the proportion of cases decided liberally, in support of civil liberties claims: from a low of less than 19 per cent in the 1946 term, when most of the issues were related to wartime repressions, increasing to around 50 per cent during the early years of the Warren Court, dipping to an unfavorable balance during the 1958–60 terms and then jumping to an average of over 76 per cent for the period since Frankfurter's de facto retirement in the spring of 1962. Prior to Frankfurter's heart attack, the pro–civil liberties rate for the 1961 term was 46 per cent; without him, the rate for the remainder of that term zoomed to 85 per cent. During the last two (the 1967 and 1968) terms of the Warren Court, 80 per cent of the civil liberties claims were decided liberally.

There have been seven major components of civil rights and liberties during the periods of the Roosevelt, Vinson, and Warren Courts: religious freedom, racial equality, civic equality, the right to privacy, voting equality, fair procedure, and political freedom. I list these in the sequence that I propose to discuss them, which corresponds to the sequence in which the Supreme Court began to give consistent and sustained support to each of these values. This by no means is the same as the order in which they appeared as issues on the Court's dockets, of course. Fair procedure cases have been considered by the Court since its beginnings in pre-John Marshall days; and it has been one hundred and thirty-six years since the Court first refused to do what it is now doing: nationalizing the entire relevant substance of the Bill of Rights. But only recently has the Court pushed aggressively to develop a national judicial policy concerning the rights of criminal defendants. Claims to racial equality were first considered in substantial numbers following the Civil War, and claims to political freedom were rarely heard by the Court until the time of World War I. Both civic equality and the right to privacy were first pressed upon the Court about a decade later, in the late twenties after Taft began to lose control over his Court. Religious freedom is an issue to which the Court gave slight consideration until the Jehovah's Witnesses began their litigious (and in general, remarkably successful) campaign in the Roosevelt Court; and voting equality did not claim the Court's attention until the end of World War II.

If we translate my analytical terms into their journalistic equivalents, they will perhaps more readily be recognized as constituting many of the most controversial of American social and political issues—or at least, they were among the most controversial until recent years, when the politics of political assassination, the fire bomb, the sit-in, and other techniques of revolutionary violence have tended to displace evolutionary politics as a method of social reform, and courts as a relevant channel for the guidance of the forces of such change. It is the more ironic, perhaps, that the Supreme Court itself has been a leading contributor to the establishment of a political milieu in which courts—including the Supreme Court—have an increasingly smaller and less relevant role to play in reshaping either the present or the future. Of course, the usual function of courts is to protect statuses quo and to forestall change; it is quite exceptional for a court to assume the position of the vanguard of the intellectual proletariat in fomenting the overthrow of the traditional order, and it is precisely because that is the social role that has been played by the United States Supreme Court, particularly under Warren, that it is important to seek to understand the causes that underlie the Warren Court's atypicality. But I wish to underscore that it is not the Warren Court's *policy activism* that makes it unique—for as we have seen, the Taft Court and the Hughes Court (to say nothing of nineteenth-century precedents) were activist, too. What distinguishes the Warren Court is its activism in behalf of the inherently contradictory libertarian goals of equalitarianism (social equality, political equality, economic equality) *and* individualism (individual rights to privacy of the mind, body, and spirit—i.e., to psychological privacy, physiological privacy, and freedom of belief).

An irony familiar to students of constitutional law is the pronounced extent to which claims to the most praiseworthy of ideals are advanced, not just often but typically, on behalf of the most blameworthy of litigants. So it was with the introduction of freedom of religion into the jurisprudence of the Supreme Court, at the behest of a proselyting association of fundamentalist, anti-Catholic, antiintellectual, antiscience, hatemongers whose own bigoted concepts of freedom of religion for themselves included zero tolerance for the beliefs or privacy otherwise of the vast majority of their non-Witness countrymen—persons who in any case were due in the none-too-distant future to be slain at Armageddon. Students of the movement have concluded that the publication activities of the national office were the fundament of the activities of the Witnesses; and beginning in the very first year of the Roosevelt Court and continuing through the end of the war, the frequently strenuous efforts of Witnesses to peddle their literature resulted in quite a few prosecutions, many of which the organization resisted by sponsoring lawsuits which they carried to the Supreme Court, where they were successful in forty-four out of a total of fifty-five cases.[73] In the process of upholding 80 per cent of the claims of the Watch Tower Bible and Tract Society, the Court also upheld a policy of loosening the restraints that many local communities in America were accustomed to place upon the interchange of religious ideas that challenged whatever might be the dominant local orthodoxies. The Witnesses's campaign was largely confined to the period of the Roosevelt Court, and it was displaced, in the Vinson Court, by a shift to two related issues of much more central concern to many more Americans: public support of Catholic education, and the integration of religious with secular education, in the public schools. There have been only two decisions on the public support issue, the first over two decades ago by the Vinson Court, for which an uniquely composed majority upheld a bus fare subsidy; and the second in June 1968 when a six-man majority of the Warren Court (over the dissents of Douglas, Fortas, and Black) upheld the New York textbook subsidy for public and private schools alike. Thus far, the Supreme Court has maintained a record of consistent approval of public fiscal support of religious education. The Vinson Court produced a pair of Janus-like decisions, the one rejecting in-school and the other approving during-but-out-of-school, released-time programs. Later came the much more clear-cut (and much more radical) policy of the Warren Court to outlaw school prayers and Bible reading, on the grounds of inescapable discrimination against individuals or minorities whose religious beliefs differed from those officially sanctioned by the exercises. But the Warren Court—and it was not the *same* Warren Court, because these decisions came before Frankfurter and Whittaker were replaced by White and Goldberg—also upheld the Sunday closing (or, blue) laws of several states, thereby sanctioning both the economic and the religious interests of the Christian majority, and rejecting the claims of such minority religious interests as those of Jews and of Seventh Day Adventists. However, on the same day that the more recent of the school prayer cases was decided, June 17, 1963, the Court began in a mild way to undercut the pro blue–law policy, by approving the claim to unemployment compensation of a Seventh Day Adventist who would not work on Saturday and was denied employment unless she would do so. Undoubtedly, what have been widely interpreted to be the "Godless" policies of the Warren Court, on the issue of freedom of religion, have been an important component among "The Causes of Popular Dissatisfaction With the Administration of Justice" (to borrow the title of Roscoe Pound's address early in this century to the American Bar Association). There have been, however, both relatively and absolutely far fewer decisions on this issue by the Warren Court, than were made by the Roosevelt and Vinson Courts together over an approximately equal period of time. The Warren Court decided one case early in 1953—a holdover from the Vinson Court that came barely six weeks after Warren was sworn in—a Jehovah's Witness claim for draft exemption, which was upheld. Eight years then elapsed before nine cases were clustered between May 1961 and June 1963, after which there were no more decisions on religious issues until the negative one in the spring of 1968. This is hardly the portrait of an activist Court soliciting litigants and pressure groups to sock it with appropriate religious issues to decide—and the techniques for doing that are well understood, and indeed well exemplified by this very issue of freedom of religion, as in the solicitation by

three members of the Roosevelt Court for an opportunity
to rectify their mistake, as they had come to view it, in the
first flag salute decision, an appeal that was promptly answered by the docketing of another case which the Court
could and did one year later, on Flag Day in 1943, decide
"rightly"—that is, in favor of school children not being
forced to bow down before graven images by saluting the
United States flag.[74] Such a deflating appraisal of the quantitative significance of the Warren Court's policies on freedom of religion—and I shall venture a qualitative appraisal,
in the third chapter, which supports the same conclusion—
may bring some comfort to any anxious citizens who are
disturbed by the possibility that the Supreme Court might
seize upon Madalyn Murray O'Hair's recent world press by-
line (and consequent litigation) in which she protested as-
tronautical recitations from Genesis, in the vicinity of the
moon. It is true that the Supreme Court seems to have been
attempting to make the Constitution follow the flag, but it
still has a long way to go before it catches up, even back here
on Earth.

If discussion of the Court's freedom of religion policies
tends to become somewhat other worldly, consideration of
what the Court has decided concerning racial equality com-
pels us to confront the core problems of a social system that
tolerated apartheid for almost three hundred years, for the
initial two centuries in the form of slavery, and for most of
the last hundred years in the form of an invidious legal discrimination that was supported by the Supreme Court's
constitutional doctrine of "separate but equal" facilities for
two segregated races, an interpretation of the Constitution
that was renounced only fifteen years ago. In my opinion,
there can be no doubt that the Warren Court's staunch advocacy of racial desegregation will prove to have been its most

55

important contribution to American public policy. It was, moreover, a change in national policy that neither the Congress nor the president could have made.[75]

The change really began during World War II, when the Roosevelt Court, in spite of its having sanctioned the racist war relocation program for West Coast Japanese Americans, reversed the Hughes Court's acquiescence in the white primary. This *volte face*, coming within less than a decade, was protested only by Roberts, the remaining member of and, indeed, the author of the majority opinion in the Court which decided the precedent decision that now was overruled. The Vinson Court soon followed up with decisions invalidating residential segregation by restrictive racial covenants and segregation in public facilities in interstate transportation, and upholding Negro claims to admission to university education on a nondiscriminatory basis. The next step was to extend the policy of nonsegregation to the nation's public schools, and this was initiated by the Vinson Court— the group of School Segregation cases already had been docketed, argued once, and scheduled for reargument before Warren's appointment. But it was the new chief justice who presided over the reargument and the rest of the Court's decision-making process; and after he had been in office barely seven months, the Court announced an unanimous decision, rejecting both state and congressional systems of segregated public education, repudiating the interpretation of the Constitution that had supported such policies, and proclaiming a national policy of racial integration that soon was to become no more acceptable to radical blacks than it previously had been to conservative whites. It was a liberal decision thrust upon a population composed mostly of people who, as the social scientists who have surveyed them tell us,[76] are not themselves liberals, but who rather tend to distrust and disbelieve egg-headed do-gooders whose interests run toward ideas and ideals rather than toward facts and realities. It was also conspicuously a policy-making decision, because the Court turned away from its precedents, purporting to rely instead upon social science research, all published within the preceding decade, by liberally-oriented sociologists and psychologists who reported what they claimed to be evidence of the deleterious effects of segregation upon education. As Warren put it, "we cannot turn the clock back . . . [and] must consider public education in the light of its full development and its present place in American life throughout the Nation." [77] The aftermath has been the extension of integration policy to include other public facilities, representation on juries, and marriage, and also the use of group tactics such as marches and sit-ins to enforce integration. Of course the Court also upheld the Twenty-fourth (anti–poll tax) Amendment and such congressional responses, to the Court's own earlier decisions, as the Civil Rights Act of 1964—in both prospective and retrospective application—and also the Civil Rights Act of 1967, and the Voting Rights Act of 1965. During the seven and a half terms beginning with White's appointment in the spring of 1962, the Court upheld claims to racial equality in thirty-five of forty-six split decisions, an approval rate of 76 per cent.

The third field of civil rights policy that the Supreme Court has developed—and contrary to the two preceding, this one can appropriately be called a policy innovation of the Warren Court—began in 1955 when an act of Congress was declared unconstitutional on the novel grounds that American civilians should not be liable to military arrest and secret deportation to overseas bases for trial by court-martial. This was only the first of a dozen invalidations of congressional legislation, within the same number of years, and all on the same issue: civic equality. Subsequent developments have included the assurance of American civilians abroad the right to trial by civilian rather than military courts, for nonmilitary offenses; the preclusion of involuntary expatriation, either as a form of punishment for military offenses or as a form of discrimination against naturalized citizens, and then (with the appointment of Fortas, who provided the fifth vote needed for a majority on the issue) a denial that Congress could on any basis expatriate a citizen, naturalized or native-born, against his consent; assurance of the right to vote of citizens literate in a language other than English; and the denial of the right of Congress to discriminate against Communist citizens by preventing them from traveling abroad. During the last seven and a half terms alone the Warren Court has upheld fifteen of twenty claims to civic equality, for an approval rate of 75 per cent.

Next comes the new constitutional right to privacy—new not as a concept of what might or what ought to be recognized as a form of constitutional right, but new in the sense that it has attracted the sustained support of the Supreme Court only since 1961. Brandeis had argued in 1928, but in dissent against a decision that went in the opposite direction, that "the makers of our Constitution . . . sought to protect Americans in their beliefs, their thoughts, their emotions and their sensations. They conferred, as against the government, the right to be let alone—the most comprehensive of rights and the right most valued by civilized men. To protect that right, every unjustifiable intrusion by the government upon the privacy of the individual, whatever the means employed, must be deemed a violation of the Fourth Amendment." [78] This was said against a federal wiretap in a prohibition enforcement case; there were of course federal search or seizure cases going back a long time before that. Beginning in the midthirties, the Hughes

Court decided an increased volume of both such Fourth Amendment claims and a new series of self-incrimination (third degree) claims by state criminal defendants. Neither the Roosevelt nor the Vinson Court upheld more than about half of such claims, however; and the first serious consideration of the possibility of nationalizing the limited concept of privacy that the Court then recognized did not come until 1949, and was rejected. There had also been a few attempts to raise questions of physiological privacy: compulsory vaccination had been upheld, early in this century, as a public health measure; and the Taft Court had upheld the sterilization of mental defectives in the name of eugenics, "in order [and I quote Holmes] to prevent our being swamped with incompetence." The Roosevelt Court did disapprove the sterilization of a recidivist chicken thief, apparently at least in part because of the lack of a clear logical nexus between the punishment—sexual impotence—and the crime—even though it was one that, according to Oklahoma, involved "moral turpitude." And the Vinson Court upheld, unanimously and on the basis of what might well be termed a gut reaction rather than an application of legal doctrine, the rejection of evidence obtained by involuntary stomach pumping as the basis for criminal conviction. But it was not until the Warren Court that even claims against *federal* search-and-seizure began to receive a consistently sympathetic hearing, with 82 per cent (fourteen of seventeen) being upheld during the first eight years of the Warren Court. In 1961 the Warren Court nationalized what it by then had begun to call the right to privacy, by declaring that it was thenceforth to be applicable to state as well as to federal criminal defendants. In subsequent decisions the Court has disapproved state anti–birth control statutes, as violations of marital privacy; and it has followed up an earlier disapproval of psychoanalytic techniques of police interrogation, with a similar disapproval of the use of narcotics—"truth serums"—as means of inducing confessions. But even the Warren Court twice has upheld sterile blood letting as a suitable means of obtaining evidence (of blood alcohol content) against suspected drunken drivers, with Brennan (for a bare majority of five in the more recent decision) giving assurances, in what can perhaps best be described as a bedside manner, that it was quite all right to force the defendant to give up his blood because "the extraction was made by a physician in a simple, medically acceptable manner in a hospital environment." [79] Moreover, as recently as the 1966 term the Warren Court rejected a majority, nine of fifteen, of the right to privacy claims, in decisions which approved the policy of basing both federal and state convictions upon evidence procured through the work of government decoys, stool pigeons, and other paid informers. During its last seven years, however, the Warren Court did uphold a majority, sixty-six of ninety-five for a rate of 69 per cent, of the right to privacy claims, including twenty-nine of thirty-four (85 per cent) during Warren's final term; and it certainly has given greater support to this value than did any earlier Court. It is nevertheless clear that even the Warren Court was not able to muster as consistent and as reliable a majority sympathetic to the right to privacy as it did in other fields of civil liberties policy.

Early in the spring of 1962 the Warren Court's decision in *Baker* v. *Carr* thrust the subject of legislative malapportionment into the forefront of national attention, and raised for widespread elite debate for the first time in American history the question of voting equality.[80] (The earlier questions of female, Negro, and youth suffrage are to be distinguished, in my opinion, because they all are concerned with the matter of voting *participation* rather than the quite different issue of *representation*.) The issue had first reached the Supreme Court sixteen years earlier, but under infortuitous circumstances with the chief justiceship vacant—Stone was dead and Vinson not yet appointed—and Jackson still away at Nuremberg; indeed, it was on the very day that the Court announced its decision in *Colegrove* v. *Green* that Jackson released to the world press his cable to the Congress, attacking President Truman for not having selected him (Jackson) as the new chief justice. The remaining justices divided 4–3 to uphold the malapportionment of the Illinois legislature, in favor of the downstate rural minority. The Vinson Court clearly opposed, in several summary *per curiam* decisions, a policy of judicial intervention; and although Brennan's appointment in 1956 gave the Warren Court a minimal majority favorable to upholding voting equality (with five of the six justices who did, in fact, comprise the majority in *Baker* v. *Carr*), the question was shouldered aside by the competitive issues of racial equality and civic equality, with which the Court then was preoccupied. But by the 1961 term several cases which raised the issue in relation to different states were docketed, and the Warren Court by then had a solid majority in favor of moving ahead with a new policy supporting legislative reapportionment. Within three years, the Court had decided thirty-two claims to the right to voting equality, and it upheld all except one. The Court has extended its policy to include both houses of state legislatures, the lower house of the Congress, and local councils of general governmental authority (such as county commissions). Most of the Warren Court's reapportionment decisions came within five years of *Baker* v. *Carr;* during the 1967 term there were only two. But the overall rate of support that the Warren Court gave to voting equality, 94 per cent (forty-six of the forty-nine cases), is the highest for any of the civil liberties components.

Frankfurter's last participation and his last dissent had

come in *Baker* v. *Carr*, against a majority that was sufficiently large and committed to push ahead in the face of
what was to be Frankfurter's last judicial gasp. With fair
procedure the equivalent move came a month later, only a
couple of weeks after Frankfurter's de facto retirement, and
when a minimal but sufficient five-man majority took ad-
vantage of an available *in forma pauperis* petition to formu-
late what is both on its face and in substance a statement of
policy for lower federal courts, concerning the right of appeal of indigent criminal defendants. It is true that *Coppedge* v. *United States*[81] had been foreshadowed by some
fourteen *per curiam* decisions strung out over the preceding
five years; but none of them had purported, nor had any
been understood, to portend a major shift in the processing
of criminal appeals. *Coppedge* did so purport; and it was
followed up by a galaxy of decisions relating to defendants
—Gideon, Escobedo, Miranda, and Gault—whose names
have become almost household words, at least in upper-
middle-class homes. Striking out over the course of the next
half-dozen years at many facets of police, prosecutory, and
judicial practices in criminal trials, both federal and state,
the general thrust of the Warren Court's fair procedure
policy has been to proclaim that society's responsibility to
criminals—most of whom are, as a class, indigent, at least
by the time of their arrest and incarceration—includes a
variety of services, aids, and assurances that affluent defendants can purchase, the better to defend against whatever
criminal charges may have been levied against them. In
effect, the costs of prosecution already had become socialized
for rich and poor alike; and according to the Court's new
policy the costs of defense also are to be socialized for the
poor, or rather, for poor criminals. The avowed justification
for the policy is to lessen the chances that the innocent will
be wrongly convicted; the necessary effect of the policy is,

of course, to make any convictions of defendants, whether innocent or guilty, more difficult to both obtain and retain. Some of the specific subcomponents of the policy include: the assurance of counsel at all major stages of the adversary process, from immediately following arrest (that is, before arraignment) to as many stages of appeal, including appeal to the Supreme Court itself, as a liberal interpretation of the claims of the defendant can justify; provision, at public expense, of copies of lower court transcripts and other parts of the case record necessary to support appeals, including a recent proviso to the effect that a state cannot deduct from a prisoner's wages the costs of a transcript provided to support an appeal; and in regard to the trial itself, the Warren Court has now read into the Fourteenth Amendment all of the key provisions of the Sixth Amendment, including (besides the right to counsel) the rights to compulsory process for obtaining witnesses in his favor, to a speedy and public trial, by an impartial jury of his economic and racial peers, to be informed of the nature and cause of the accusation, and to be confronted with witnesses against him. The Eighth Amendment, prohibiting cruel and unusual punishment, is already nationalized and may yet (notwithstanding the replacement of Warren and Fortas) be further extended by a Supreme Court decision within the next decade holding that capital punishment by either the federal or state governments no longer comports with civilized standards of decency and humaneness.[82] This means that of the substantive Bill of Rights (that is, the first eight amendments), the first, fourth, sixth, and eighth all have become nationalized —the fourth, sixth, and eighth by the Warren Court, and the first earlier. No person in his right mind would wish to extend further, in our contemporary urban and industrial society, the right to bear arms—as Cliff Grant has observed, "we need a liberally construed second amendment as a limitation on the states about as badly as a hole in the head —indeed the two might go together," [83] nor would any sane state government now want to quarter troops in private dwellings, in peace or war. So the course of both wisdom and virtue may well lie in *not* nationalizing the second and third amendments, Hugo Black to the contrary notwithstanding.[84] A guarantee of jury trial in suits at common law for an amount of twenty dollars or more would also be a dubious innovation to thrust upon state courts, so we can perhaps forget about the seventh, too. This leaves only the Fifth Amendment; and here also there are both theoretical and practical problems in the path of the course of "full incorporation" for which both Justices Black and Douglas have so long argued. To enforce the grand jury system upon all of the states today is so reactionary a step that, so far as I am aware, no well-informed person has seriously proposed it, at least in modern times; the self-incrimination clause already has been incorporated in the new right to privacy, as we have seen, with the incidental by-product of the coining of another household phrase—"to take the Fifth"; the due process clause already is iterated in the Fourteenth Amendment; and this leaves us with double jeopardy, the one conspicuously laggard sector in the Warren Court's development of a policy of promoting fair procedure. In thirteen decisions over the course of a dozen years beginning in 1957, the Warren Court had upheld only four double jeopardy claims, for a support rate of 31 per cent; but on the closing day of its existence, Warren's Court upheld two more and announced the triumphant (if belated) overruling of *Palko*, and the incorporation of double jeopardy as an aspect of fair procedure that the states should respect.[85]

There is also one aspect of criminal trial procedure, relating to juvenile defendants, in which the Warren Court took what only a few years ago would have been regarded as a highly retrogressive step. It was precisely in response to the advice of social scientists, and as a result of a conscious preference for rehabilitative in place of punitive theories about the trial of young offenders, that specialized juvenile courts were established, given exclusive jurisdiction over the offenses of children and younger adolescents, and the authority to function without publicity and without adversary conflict between opposing lawyers—the judge of the juvenile court was supposed to be a person primarily interested in the problems of maladjusted or mistreated young people, and it was assumed that he could be presumed to safeguard the interests of the accused better than could be accomplished by having the defendant represented by counsel. Against this background, the Warren Court's pronouncement that juveniles are entitled to the panoply of basic components that comprise adult adversary due process—which were defined as including notice, counsel, confrontation, cross-examination, privilege against self-incrimination, transcript rights, and appeal—can only be regarded as a victory for majority sentiment in the organized legal profession, and as a major defeat for the progressive views that had been sponsored by an earlier generation of social reformers and their sociologist acolytes. Certainly this policy of the Warren Court ought to be viewed as evidence of the Court's consistency in technique, while at the same time giving heart to those conservatives who had thought that the Warren Court was liberal about everything. Any Court that loves kids that much can't be all good.

Political freedom is in several respects the core issue of civil libertarianism. It was through the confrontation, by the White and Taft and Hughes Courts, with the claims of sundry Communists, anarchists, labor leaders, and protofascists, that the Supreme Court first became engaged, in the period between the two world wars, with the more general problems of civil liberties in regard to which the Warren Court has been so conspicuously active. The Roosevelt Court established and the Vinson Court continued a policy of upholding newspaper editorial commentary upon pending trials, and of disapproving judicial censorship of the press. The Roosevelt Court also initiated the first of what has since become the Supreme Court's repeated forays into the marketplace of ideas and tastes, for the purpose of liberalizing the exchange of opinions concerning both art and politics. Both issues—obscenity and censorship—were joined in this pilot case, which concerned the mailability of a magazine that can perhaps best be described as *Playboy*'s intellectual great-godfather, if one compares George Petty's lithesome cartoons with the playmate-of-the-month. The objectionable features in *Esquire* were said to reflect (and I quote Justice Douglas directly on this) "the smoking-room type of humor, featuring, in the main, sex." The Vinson Court's only relevant contribution to this issue was to uphold the distribution of magazines (and again I quote) "made up principally of stories of deeds of bloodshed, lust, or crime" while rejecting the distribution of a collection of short stories by the country's then most eminent literary critic. The Vinson Court subsequently did, however, approve the exhibition of Roberto Rosselini's *Ways of Love* (a trilogy including "The Miracle," which the New York censor had declared to be sacrilegious). But it was not until 1957 that the Warren Court began to process cases in sufficient numbers to begin to lay down a policy. And at that time, less than a dozen years ago, the Court upheld the censorship of some paperbacks that evidently were deemed to be sadistic, and the convictions, variously under state and federal law, of distributors of what were described as obscene books, photographs, and magazines. In the process of justifying these results, the Court made one of its lesser contributions to cognitive clarity, by explaining that what obscenity really means is prurience, and then citing Webster's *New International* as a precedent on prurience. (This might have provided a more useful guide, were it not for the circumstance that the definition in Webster is tautological.) Since then, the Warren Court has upheld, against both censorship and findings of obscenity, most of the dozen or so claims that it has considered, accepting works that had passed into academic repertoires of literature (such as *Lady Chatterley* and *Fanny Hill*) and a good many more that have not, on the whole, as yet achieved such status (and one thinks here of such books as *Passion Slave*, or *The Wife-Swappers*, the advertising for which proclaimed that it is "So Vile It will Stun You"). Standards that certainly are unascertainable, and that may well also be unattainable, were in 1965 posited by the Court as necessary to justify movie censorship; although in the following year convictions for what the Court called pandering were upheld in both state and federal prosecutions. With the latter pair of decisions the Warren Court seemed from a doctrinal point of view to have come full circle, right back where it began nine years earlier, condemning prurience but nothing else, and even with the same voting division except that Stewart, who had replaced Whittaker in the interim, joined the dissenters. But of course, the Court had in the meantime supplied many examples of what it meant by nonprurience; and the tastes and practices of consumers of freedom of expression certainly had become much less restrained than had been the case theretofore.[86]

The other major aspect of freedom of expression, the right to articulate political dissent, has had its ups and downs, at the hands of the Supreme Court, during the past thirty years. The early part of the Roosevelt Court was an "up" period; but this was quickly cut off by World War II, which was down; then the immediate postwar period, the first three terms of the Vinson Court, was another brief interval sympathetic to political debate; but again, a dramatic truncation occurred in 1949, due jointly to personnel changes and the ascendancy of Senator Joseph McCarthy, inaugurating another era of unfavorable decisions that lasted until the mid-fifties, when the appointments of Warren and Brennan made it possible for favorable majorities to form once again, as they began to do in almost wholesale fashion in 1957 and early 1958. This led to a direct congressional reaction, during the waning years of the Eisenhower administration, and to explicit statutory proposals to amend and curtail the Court's jurisdiction. These were defeated; but as in 1937, so once again did the Court "reform" itself —in a series of five to four decisions in which the Court's former majority was converted into a minority on issues of political freedom, because—and explicitly because—Frankfurter switched.[87] The consequence was another, but this time much briefer, period of unfavorable decisions, lasting from 1959 until Frankfurter's retirement three years later. The Warren Court's general record of support over the past seven and a half terms, for claims of political freedom, was an average of 76 per cent (fifty-six of seventy-four decisions).

Frankfurter's replacement by Goldberg reinstated the former majority and their policy of upholding freedom in political communications. Since then the Warren Court has broadened and deepened its support, extending it to include defendants before legislative investigating committees (both congressional and state); the invalidation of loyalty oaths for teachers; membership as well as leadership in the Communist party; the right of Communists to serve as officers of labor unions, and also to receive Communist propaganda through the mail; and then in 1965, fifteen years after the

Internal Security Act was adopted and a dozen years after the Subversive Activities Control Board had duly found the Communist party of the United States to be a "Communist-action organization" within the meaning of the statute and therefore bound to register under it, and in the Court's third decision in the case (which had made prior full dress appearances in 1956 and 1961), the Court finally decided that this aspect of the statute was unconstitutional. The Communist labor leaders and Communist mailings issues also involved declarations of unconstitutionality of acts of Congress; and the latter was the first time that the Supreme Court had ever declared a congressional statute in conflict with the First Amendment.[88] Even the Warren Court was not willing to encourage the exercise of the rights of assembly and petition, however, when these took the form of picketing and lobbying and trespassing around jails and courthouses;[89] and the Court backed up an injunction to prevent a civil rights march in Birmingham, by upholding the demonstrators' convictions for contempt of court. The supporting majority opinion failed to clarify how and why judicial intervention in economic disputes, by means of the labor injunction, was an illiberal kind of judicial activism, while judicial intervention in political disputes, by means of the civil rights injunction, was not so. Indeed, neither the Vinson nor the early Warren Court was particularly sympathetic to defendants who had been summarily convicted for contempt of judges;[90] and it was not until June 1968 that the Warren Court announced that at least those "serious" judicial or legislative criminal contempts that entail two-year jail sentences are entitled (like misdemeanors subject to equivalent punishment) to trial by jury.

Spaeth has pointed out that during the five-year period of the 1960–64 terms, the Warren Court upheld only 54 per cent (44 of 81) of the civil liberties claims against the national government, while upholding the much higher rate of 75 per cent (85 of 115) against the states. Moreover, the differential seemed to cut across the range of civil liberties issues, as I have described them here; for example, during this same period 42 per cent (8 of 19) of the right to privacy claims against the national government were upheld, while 65 per cent (41 of 63) were upheld against the states.[91] This finding flatly contradicts legal dogma, including the Court's own orthodoxy, which holds that the national government is "more closely confined" by the explicit language of the Bill of Rights, whereas the states are left with greater discretion because of the looser language of the Fourteenth Amendment. But it is doubtful if any incumbent member of the Court, with the possible exception of Harlan who continues to preach it, still believes in this fiction of the Taft and Hughes Courts. As Krislov has pointed out, "This finding is perhaps, legally speaking, surprising, in view of the principles of state autonomy and standards of federalism and the supposedly greater supervisory power of the Supreme Court over federal courts. But it will hardly surprise those conversant with the realities of civil liberties. The tough cases raising issues of fluctuating legal standards or highly subjective judgments generally originate in local transactions; and, in any event, state courts are less sensitive to federal standards."[92] And Spaeth's conclusion, after a careful analysis of the matter, is that "considerations of federalism are simply irrelevant as motivators of judicial behavior in the field of civil rights and liberties, and . . . the greater frequency of Court support for the national government rather than state governments in civil-liberty cases results from the view that state protection of civil liberties and state standards of law enforcement are inferior to those of the national government."[93]

Overall, the Warren Court in the sixties most consistently

supported claims to voting equality, with a rate of 94 per cent; it gave least consistent support to privacy, at about 69 per cent; and the remaining five civil liberties values—religious freedom, fair procedure, racial equality, civic equality, and political freedom—all fared the same, ranging from 75 to 80 per cent.

It seems clear that, in relation to its predecessors, Warren's was the most activist court not only in American, but with a high degree of probability, also in world history, in regard alike to the number and the diversity of the civil libertarian causes that it sponsored, and the degree of favorable support that it gave to such causes. We have seen, however, that whereas the shift away from economic activism by the Hughes Court was a sharp and dramatic reversal, in which the Court turned its back upon one political role and openly embraced an alternative one to which it has remained faithful for a period of over thirty years, the construction of an activist role toward civil liberties policy has been a work of gradual development over the full course of the past half century, with some backsliding and false starts, but on the whole a record of steady, consistent progress toward a developing concept of greater human freedom and equality, and of more democratic participation in decision making. And the Warren Court went much further than had proved possible for either the Roosevelt or the Vinson Court, both in limiting to a relatively small sphere its participation in economic policy making, and also in putting and keeping pressure for social and political reform upon the rest of the national government, the state judiciaries, and American society. But one naturally wonders why it is that a group of middle-aging to elderly lawyer-politicians should have chosen to play such a role, at this time and in this country; and what effect their efforts have had, upon the behaviors of their countrymen. Those are the two questions that I shall discuss in the two chapters that follow.

CHAPTER II

CONSTITUTIONAL
POLITICS

"If five lawyers," said the chief justice of North Carolina, at the turn of the century, "can negative the will of one hundred million men, then the art of government is reduced to the selection of those five lawyers." [1] Walter Clark's way of putting the matter tends, perhaps, to oversimplify things somewhat; but his point is clear enough. Thirty-eight lawyers have in fact served on the Supreme Court during the past half century, and our task in this chapter will be to attempt to appraise the ways, relevant to their attempts to influence the running of the country, in which they were similar to and different from each other.

It is a far cry, in American politics, from the days of Warren Harding's front-porch campaign to the Nixon TV spectaculars, such as the show in which he introduced the 1969 Republican cabinet to his countrymen—indeed, to much of the world, by grace of satellite transmission. As a group, they were elderly, white, male, and mostly lawyers— a description that would have done equally well to characterize the Harding cabinet. No doubt if the opportunities for service in the cabinet and in the Court were equivalent, it would be possible to make a similar statement about the similiarity between the Supreme Court today and the Court in Harding's day. It is precisely because the American constitutional system is sufficiently *un*democratic, so that the Supreme Court can and often does differ (and for extended periods of time) in its policy preferences from those of the incumbent national administration, that it is important for us to attempt to reappraise the kind of effect that changes in the American political culture have had upon the Supreme Court.

The Nixon cabinet was notorious, even before its unveiling (if that is the right participle to describe the process), for its failure to include any (and in this order of perceived importance) Negroes, Democrats, or women. Quite to the contrary, the lame-duck Supreme Court (as it necessarily was perceived to be early in 1969, from the standpoint of the incoming president) included twice as many Democrats as Republicans, and there was by then one Negro member of the Court. It took the entire period of our constitutional experience to date to create the political climate of opinion in which it was possible to put a black in that august assembly, but the important thing is that he is there now. There may even be some hope, however slight, for sexual emancipation to reach such extremes that a female justice can be appointed some day. It has, after all, proved possible for two Catholics (White and McKenna) to sit together on the Court for over a decade, and for two Jews (Brandeis and Cardozo) to do so for half a dozen years, without apparent damage to the Court's institutional integrity. It is true that the coexistence on the Court of Brandeis and Cardozo had an important effect upon the Court's policy development in the early thirties, but the effect was a continuation of the one that Brandeis had been producing in company with Cardozo's predecessor, Holmes—and Holmes

himself was a person conspicuously unconcerned with religious affiliations or dogmas.

Throughout this work I shall continue to make use of the
concepts "liberal" and "conservative," relating these to policy
positions on the same issues covered in Chapter I, where
these issues were described in terms of the extent to which
the Supreme Court upheld, in its decisions, outcomes that
were liberal or conservative. But these concepts also define
stable, crucial, and enduring ideological differences among
Supreme Court justices that not only are meaningful, but
indeed are indispensable to any comprehensive analysis of
the Court's role and work. Because my view of this matter
differs sharply from that which has been adopted by many
(if not most) of my distinguished predecessors in the Gaspar G. Bacon Lectureship, I feel compelled to be quite explicit about this difference, rather than to gloss over it *sub
silentio*. Mason, for example, has said of the Taft Court:
"The handy labels 'liberal' and 'conservative' mistake the
underlying basis of the cleavage. Conservatives all, the
division among the Justices was rooted in fundamental differences as to the nature of the judicial function"; and
Pritchett has referred to "the contrasting complexes of attitudes and values which go by the confusing tags of liberalism
and conservatism." [2] Both Mason and Pritchett are scholars
who have made an important contribution to our understanding of the political role of the Supreme Court—and
certainly both are men upon whose work I myself have relied heavily in the very task of preparing the present volume.
Both wrote, however, before the publication, during the past
decade, of a considerable amount of research into the social
psychology of judicial ideology, attitudes, values, and decisional behavior. Of course Mason is right when he says that
all members of the Taft Court, including Brandeis and

Holmes and Stone, were (like F.D.R. himself, as Mason points out)[3] conservatives—they were, that is, if we postulate the late Norman Thomas as our criterion of liberalism. On the other hand, as compared to Stephen J. Field, all were liberals. But comparison with Thomas or Field is relevant, for present purposes, only to provide perspective. What is more relevant is to know that on almost every issue that came before the Taft Court, when division did occur Clarke and Brandeis and Holmes and Stone were consistently more liberal, all of them, than were Sanford, Taft, Sutherland, Van Devanter, Butler, or McReynolds; and that in the Hughes Court, Cardozo and Stone and Brandeis and Holmes were more liberal, across the same broad range of issues, than were Hughes and Roberts, who in turn were more liberal across these same issues than were Sutherland, Van Devanter, Butler, or McReynolds. The relative division between Brandeis and Stone, on the other hand, and the Sutherland-Van Devanter-Butler-McReynolds group, on the other, persisted throughout the two decades. Similarly, since the late thirties consistent differences in regard to issues of social, economic, and political policy can be observed both within and between groups consisting of, on the one hand, liberals such as Murphy, Rutledge, Douglas, Black, Fortas, Warren, Brennan, Marshall, and Goldberg—Black, subject to a recent caveat that I shall discuss—and on the other hand the remaining justices who have served in the past three decades. The economically liberal position has meant to uphold, first, government ownership and operation of public services; second, governmental regulation and taxation—both national and state—of business enterprise; third, the claims of unions in disputes with employers; and fourth, the fiscal claims of economic inferiors (such as injured workmen against their employers, widows against insurance companies, and injured passengers against transportation car-

riers). Political liberalism has meant to uphold the claims
to equality of relatively disadvantaged minorities, irrespective whether the line of division be race, sex, citizenship, or
legislative representation; to uphold the claims to fair procedure of criminal defendants, irrespective whether the prosecutor be federal or state; to uphold freedom of speech,
press, assembly, religion, and the separation of church and
state; and to uphold the right to privacy, irrespective whether the issue be cast in the classical legal forms of the
Fourth Amendment or the self-incrimination clause of the
Fifth, or in the more novel guise of electronic surveillance,
narcotic manipulation, or surgical transformation of human
physiological or psychological processes.[4] It is these substantive policy issues of contemporary politics, and therefore of
contemporary liberalism and conservatism, and not primarily
differences in judicial role conceptions, that have divided the
Court. The differences in role concepts have been important,
but not as the cause of differences among the justices; rather,
the talk about role concepts (viz., activism and restraint)
has served as a smokescreen to disguise and cover up the
tracks of the underlying substantive ideological differences.
The tags are confusing only to the extent that one's method
of analysis precludes his ever getting beyond the surface level
of manifest variance, for it certainly is true that liberal and
conservative do not describe a single dimension of differences
among the Supreme Court justices of whom I shall speak.
But they do describe a limited and manageably small array
of issues; and the task of useful analysis becomes to denote
the pattern of interrelations among issues, and then to apply
this analytic framework consistently throughout the period of
time one seeks to appraise, as I attempted to do in the first
chapter. Of course, I should not presume to deny the possibility that, at some future time, the extension of currently
popular radical orientations may render inappropriate, as a

set of concepts for analyzing the Supreme Court, liberal-conservative ideology; but such a development necessarily lies, if at all, in the future. Many of us know colleagues and students who can best be described as radical (rather than as liberal or conservative) in their political, social, and (to a lesser extent) economic orientations. As yet, however, no radical has been appointed to the Supreme Court, with the possible exception of William O. Douglas.[5]

It is customary, when speaking of eras in the development of constitutional policy by the Supreme Court, to refer to different periods by using the name of the incumbent chief justice—thus, we speak of the Marshall Court, the Taney Court, and the Warren Court. I follow this particular custom, and for what I think are very good reasons. The chief is more than *primus inter pares,* and with rare exceptions he has been considerably more than that throughout the nineteenth and the present centuries. He votes as an equal, but he controls the agenda of the conference, he directs discussion, he speaks first and votes last; the initial (and primary) evaluation of jurisdictional decisions is done under his supervision; when voting with the majority he assigns the writing of majority opinions among the associates; he presides in open Court (e.g., over oral argument, and over the reading of opinion summaries on decision days); he has been for over a century now the Chief Justice of the United States—not only of the Supreme Court—with extensive supervisory responsibilities over the entire—and certainly it can now be said with considerable justification, the sprawling—federal judicial system; and for most Americans (and for many observers abroad) who have any awareness of the existence of the United States Supreme Court, it is the chief justice who symbolizes—indeed, who personifies—that court as a curiously human, yet (in terms of its reputed authority and influence) almost superhuman, institution.

CONSTITUTIONAL POLITICS

I shall focus on the past five decades, beginning with the appointment of William Howard Taft, and extending up to mid-1969. Taft was chief justice throughout the twenties, and Earl Warren was chief for a decade and a half, from the early days of the Eisenhower administration through the first half year under Nixon. Between Taft and Warren came Charles Evans Hughes, who served throughout the thirties; Harlan Fiske Stone, who headed the Court during World War II; and Fred Vinson, whose seven years in the Marble Palace were in close phase with the occupancy of the nearby White House by his selector, Harry S Truman. Vinson was the only Democrat among these five chiefs; and therefore except for him, the chief justice of the United States for over forty of the past forty-eight years has been a Republican, a trend that has been reinforced by the appointment of Warren Burger to replace Earl Warren. During this same period, however, a majority of the associate justices were Democrats, reflecting (much better than did the office of the chief) the preponderant control over the presidency that the Democratic party has exercised. Of these four Republicans, one (Warren) had been a candidate for the presidency; another (Hughes) had been his party's nominee for the presidency; and a third (Taft) had been president. (Indeed, Taft and Hughes had taken turns in running as the major opponent to Woodrow Wilson.) It takes a high degree of politicization to emerge as a man who is both available and eligible for the presidency; and these three politicos among them held down the center chair on the Supreme Court for thirty-five years. All three of them had had considerable other administrative experience as well: Warren as governor and as attorney general of California, Hughes as governor of New York and as Harding's secretary of state, and Taft as governor of the Philippines and as Theodore Roosevelt's secretary of war. Moreover, two of these four Republican chief justices, viewed collectively, were also exceptionally endowed with prior judicial experience as associate members of the Supreme Court: there have been only three chiefs, in our entire history, who have had such previous experience, including Hughes (whom Taft had appointed as an associate justice in 1910, in part to eliminate him as a potential rival for the Republican presidential nomination in 1912) and Stone (who had served as an associate justice under both Taft and Hughes).

The Taft Court

When William Howard Taft took over the supervision of the Supreme Court from Edward Douglass White, a former Confederate lieutenant who had grown up on a sugar plantation run by slave labor, no great change was apparent in the kinds of policy results supported in the Court's decisions. And why should there have been? Taft himself had picked White for the job, partly because of his confidence (notwithstanding the circumstance that Taft himself was a Protestant Republican Northerner while White was a Catholic Democratic Southerner) that White would vote the right way on the important issues likely to confront the Court; [6] and partly because White was sufficiently old (sixty-five) at the time Taft promoted him to the center chair that Taft, a dozen years younger, could (as he most certainly in fact did come to do) look forward to nature taking its course (even if understandings between humans should fail) so that a vacancy could be anticipated in the chief justiceship by the time Taft was himself available to fill it. [7]

Once he was finally in the role that had been the openly avowed object of his ambition throughout most of his lifetime, Taft played it for all it was worth, lobbying with considerable success throughout the government (and country) to control appointments to his Court; [8] working within the Court to maximize the group's support for his own value preferences; and virtually single-handedly arranging to have drafted, and lobbying through Congress, the changes in federal judicial organization and procedure that made Taft in fact the first chief justice of the federal judiciary as the presiding officer of an annual national policy-making judicial conference, and that gave his Court the right, thenceforth, to pick and choose which cases and issues it would act upon.[9] A combination of old age and what proved to be a mistaken judgment about the fourth and final personnel addition to his Court (Stone) resulted in a gradual loss in Taft's grip over his "team" (as he liked to call it), particularly during his last three years; but during his first half dozen or so years, Taft did remarkably well in translating the Constitution into an image closer to his heart's desire. The man was a virtual judicial Stakhanovite: between 1921 and 1928, he averaged thirty opinions per term, 50 per cent more than the average for his associates, and this notwithstanding his reluctance to articulate dissent—or to have anybody else do so either, for that matter—from an opinion that was acceptable to a majority. Hughes has reported that Taft dissented only seventeen times in ten years, and in only three of these instances did Taft himself write the dissenting opinion; [10] and Danelski has revealed that the Taft Court suppressed, during this same period, over two hundred dissenting votes.[11] However, with his Court deciding an average of over three hundred cases per term, Taft evidently was still in actual agreement with the decision over 93 per cent of the time, as well as being in apparent agreement well over 99 per cent of the time. Moreover, practically all of those thirty opinions per term that he wrote—again, 99 per cent of them—were unanimous or majority opinions in which Taft spoke in the name of his Court.

Although Taft was on the conservative side of almost every split civil liberties decision of his Court [12] and the author of many of his Court's best-known, and most conservative, majority opinions on economic policy, there were at least a few matters concerning which he had become enlightened: he understood something about the problems of working conditions in southern textile mills, and about munitions production, as the direct result of his World War I experience as chairman of the National War Labor Board, during which he had presided over extensive hearings on those two subjects.[13] And quite unlike Brandeis, or Holmes, Taft had a soft spot for women and children. One of his three dissenting opinions came in a case involving emergency war administration and presidential wartime delegation.[14] Another came in *Adkins* v. *Children's Hospital*,[15] where the majority declared unconstitutional a congressional minimum wage law for women and children. Other and characteristic underdog dissenting votes by Taft were against the majority's refusal to award compensation to the parents of children drowned in a poisoned pool, and against the majority's refusal to uphold the conviction of a father who refused to support his young daughters.[16] It is notable, too, that one of the very few unanimous decisions of the Taft Court in *support* of socioeconomic reform came in *Massachusetts* v. *Mellon*,[17] which upheld an early federal grant-in-aid program for maternal and infant health and welfare. Taft was also a staunch advocate of the World Court, although no case came along providing him with an opportunity to write in support of that issue.

When Taft joined the Court in 1921, two of his associates, Willis Van Devanter and Mahlon Pitney, were Republicans whom he himself had appointed a decade earlier. Van Devanter was a Wyoming railroad lawyer, who had also served as both the chief justice of the state supreme court and as a federal circuit judge; Pitney was a second-generation lawyer and an antilabor New Jersey state judge, former congressman, and leader in the state senate and in state Republican politics. Two other Republicans, Holmes and William Day, were the choices of Teddy Roosevelt. Day, a crony of McKinley, was secretary of state during the Spanish-American War and subsequently Taft's colleague as a federal circuit judge. McKinley's only appointee to the Supreme Court, Joseph McKenna, a California Republican and the third Roman Catholic to reach the Court, was the senior associate justice with twenty-three years of service when Taft took over. McKenna was a former federal circuit judge, and congressman (and one of the few who voted against the establishment of the Interstate Commerce Commission), an intimate of Leland Stanford and of William McKinley (whose attorney general he had been), and reputedly a great friend of the Southern Pacific Railway. The remaining three justices were all Wilson men: James McReynolds, a Tennessee Democrat, was a law professor who had been in charge of antitrust prosecutions for Roosevelt, and who subsequently was attorney general under Wilson. Louis Brandeis was a progressive Republican, an exceptionally successful and well-to-do Boston lawyer whose appointment had been bitterly contested in the Senate (by, among others, Taft himself, and Sutherland), because of the progressive proconsumer and proworkingmen causes that he had supported. John Clarke was a Democrat and Ohio politician, the son of an Irish immigrant, a successful Cleveland corporation lawyer, the lifelong friend of Newton D. Baker (Wilson's secretary of war) and a political enemy of Marc Hanna (who came from the same home town).

During Taft's first two years, his Court was a balanced one, with a conservative bloc of only three—McReynolds to Taft's right and Van Devanter on Taft's left—with Day and McKenna next, in the center; then Holmes, just slightly left of center, and finally a three-man liberal bloc: Clarke, Brandeis, and Pitney, in that order. There were, of course, many issues on which Taft's Court was in substantial agreement, or at least in sufficient agreement that compromise could lead to the repression of whatever differences in view may initially have been expressed in conference discussion and memoranda. But when divergence was too great for unanimity to be achieved, the early Taft Court characteristically was arrayed in the sequence that I have specified, for both economic and civil liberties questions. There is not the slightest basis for doubt that McReynold's position represented the most conservative point on the scale that I have indicated; neither can there be any doubt that John Clarke represented such an extremely liberal position—he was the very first modern liberal justice to be appointed—that, when he resigned in 1922 to spend his time (more fruitfully, as he thought) campaigning for world peace, his ideological place remained vacant until Franklin Roosevelt appointed William Douglas, sixteen years later.

Clarke's decision to quit was an event that had exceptional implications for the development of both the Supreme Court and the country. Clarke had served for only six years, and he lived on for another twenty-three, until the end of World War II. He was a strong supporter of the New Deal, and he stood behind the president in his proposal to pack the Court—although Clarke did *not* approve of Roberts's switch. Clarke liked Stone's decisions, welcomed Frankfurter's appointment, and thought so highly of Robert Jackson's *The Struggle for Judicial Supremacy* that he personally recommended the book to F.D.R.[18] Clarke's presence and his voice on the Court would have been of great importance, if he had served for another decade and a half until F.D.R.'s second term began, or even if he had resigned during Roosevelt's first term, thereby providing the opportunity that never in fact arose for F.D.R. to make an early appointment to the Court. The difference would have been important because Clarke's replacement was George Sutherland, a United States senator and former American Bar Association president whose English parents had pioneered in the Utah Territory and whose appointment was the payoff of a political debt—he had been Harding's campaign manager. Sutherland at once joined forces with McReynolds, Taft, and Van Devanter to form the conservative bloc that dominated the Supreme Court for the next fifteen years. Indeed, it was a majority conservative bloc after Butler was appointed in the following year, 1923, until Taft's death in 1930. Thereafter, stigmatized by liberal critics as the "Four Horsemen," the group was primarily responsible for determining the Court's policy course during the critical years of the New Deal. But old age finally eliminated this septuagenarian bloc, as Van Devanter retired (but only *after* the Court-packing struggle) at the age of seventy-eight in 1937, Sutherland at seventy-six the following year, and Butler died at seventy-three in 1939, leaving only McReynolds to call it quits at the age of seventy-nine in 1941.

If Clarke had chosen to stick it out on the Court, there could have been no majority conservative bloc for Taft to lead; instead, Taft would have presided over a balanced Court, with a four-man liberal bloc (Clarke, Brandeis, Holmes, and Stone) serving as a counterpoise to his conservative bloc, and with the moderately conservative Sanford in the middle. It would still have been, as Mason says, a conservative Court; but it would have been a far less conservative one than it became, in fact, with George Sutherland ensconced in John Clarke's seat. More than likely, the transition to the Roosevelt Court and the modern period of the Court's jurisprudence would have come sooner, and without the political struggle with Roosevelt, because Hughes would have returned in 1930 to preside over a Court that leaned to the left instead of to the right; and for anyone as political as Hughes, that would have made all the difference. What the effect might have been, if Roosevelt's second term had concentrated upon additional nonemergency legislation for domestic social and economic reform, instead of a dissipating fight with the Supreme Court, we can only dimly imagine now. But to get a better notion of what difference it did make, to have Sutherland in and Clarke out, let us suppose the converse: that Bill Douglas, instead of James Byrnes, resigned in 1942 to become "assistant president" as director of economic stabilization in the war emergency administration, and that in place of Douglas, F.D.R. had promoted (in the name of party and wartime harmony) Joseph C. Hutcheson, Jr., the longtime district and circuit and sometime chief judge of the Fifth United States Court of Appeals (1918–1964), both a proponent and an exponent of realist jurisprudence,[19] and a Southern Democrat who when McCarthyism was rampant boasted he was "a Jeffersonian, Lincolnian American" with but slight sympathy for "the sophisticated positivists, the skeptical pragmatists, the creeping socialists, and the social planners of all shades" who, regretably, had come to dominate the work of the Supreme Court.[20] The Hutch (as he was affectionately called) certainly was an available choice for a job on the Court; and if appointed instead of Douglas, either in 1939 or three years later, he would have been the most conservative justice on either the Roosevelt, the Vinson, or the Warren Courts, and the only one to represent the older, pre–New Deal conservative point of view. Without

Douglas but with Hutcheson, there would not even have been four liberal votes on the Court at the same time to control jurisdictional grants until Goldberg joined the Court in 1962; and there would have been no liberal majority on the merits at any time since the establishment of the Court in 1790, because, by the time Thurgood Marshall reached the Court in 1967, Hugo Black had relapsed to such an extent that he could no longer be considered a supporter of most liberal causes. The entire thrust of the Warren Court's civil libertarian policy innovations would have been very different. Hutcheson's appointment would have been a catastrophe, from the liberal point of view; and Clarke's resignation was catastrophic, for the same reason.

As it was, instead, the conservative Pierce Butler replaced the moderate Day, and the moderate conservative Sanford replaced the moderate liberal Pitney—both further net losses for liberal representation on the Court, leaving it with only Brandeis on the left, Holmes slightly left of center, Sanford and McKenna in the middle, and then the more conservative justices—Butler, Van Devanter, Taft, Sutherland, and McReynolds. Butler was an Irish Democrat and Roman Catholic, and the Taft Court's only member to come from a working-class social background; but he was also a railroad lawyer, and Taft had worked hard to assure his selection.[21] The appointment was, in many respects, a rerun of Taft's earlier elevation of White—an ostentatiously broadminded move, across both partisan and religious lines, but perfectly safe to make because of the assurance of the ideological suitability of the candidate. Edward Sanford was a Tennessee Republican who had been put on the federal district bench by Teddy Roosevelt, and promoted by Harding as a safe alternative to such more distinguished other possibilities as Benjamin Cardozo and Learned Hand. In practice, the potentially solid right-wing majority bloc did not form during the 1923 and 1924 terms, probably because the opposition—now reduced to Brandeis and Holmes —was too weak, at least in terms of votes; instead, a more moderate coalition of the center-right, ranging from Sanford through Taft, became the dominant subgroup at this time, leaving both Sutherland and McReynolds as the occasional right-wing dissenters, just as Brandeis and Holmes occasionally dissented on the left. The addition of Sanford, had, in effect, co-opted McKenna into the majority group, while squeezing McReynolds out; so the effect of the liquidation of the Taft Court's fleeting liberal bloc was to ameliorate, at least temporarily, the tendency toward ideological bifurcation that became accentuated after 1930, resulting in the dramatic events of 1937.

McKenna was the next to go: during at least the period of the 1923 and 1924 terms, he was persisting in the senile ambition to outlast Holmes, although he had become so incompetent that he managed to write an opinion justifying a decision opposite to what had been agreed to unanimously (including himself) in conference.[22] McKenna was replaced by Harlan Stone, Coolidge's attorney general and a Republican, the former dean of the Columbia Law School, and a member of a Wall Street firm that was counsel for the J. P. Morgan interests. As a justice of the Supreme Court, Stone initially took a position only slightly to the left of center, between Sanford and Holmes; and for the next five years, the Taft Court remained dominated by a majority bloc of the center-right, but a more conservative one than during 1923 and 1924 because it included Sutherland in lieu of McKenna, and also McReynolds on the far right. This left a loosely knit liberal bloc consisting of Brandeis on the far left, and Holmes and Stone closer to the middle.

There was also a second qualitative difference in the Taft Court after 1925. Taft increasingly experienced less success in his unremitting efforts to "mass the Court" in team performances of unanimity, and for three reasons. First, both he and Van Devanter began to experience more and more the sheer physical effects of aging, such as the debilitating effect of illness and the annoyance of forgetfulness. Second, and closely related, is the hardening of the intellectual arteries which, in Taft's case, meant that a conservative political philosophy tempered by considerable social grace and personal good will deteriorated, in his final year or two on the Court, into what was a form of near paranoia, concerning both his more liberal associates and his countrymen. Third, Stone's co-option by Brandeis and Holmes meant that Taft's majority bloc had an opposition too large to be glossed over or ignored, and this meant considerably more give and take within the group than had theretofore been necessary—and it came at a time when Taft himself was becoming less and less fit to engage in such political work.

The main reason for the Taft Court's conservative decisional policies—which we have examined in terms of their value content—is, of course, that Taft himself and a solid majority of his colleagues were men with what were even for their day quite conservative value preferences—and that assertion is no tautology: there is ample evidence, independent of any of the Taft Court's decisions, to support it.[23] Moreover, we know the basic reason why there were so many conservatives on the Taft Court: it was because many people were tired of fighting World War I, suspicious of Wilson's League, and anxious for a return to normalcy in the domestic economy. They got it, and in the instance of the Supreme Court, they got their money's worth. If circumstances had been significantly different, and if Cox could have been elected president in 1920, then it would have been likely that Cardozo or Learned Hand would have become chief justice instead of Taft. Clearly, White's resignation had left the Court with neither a liberal nor a conservative bias; but the successive appointments of Taft, Sutherland, and Butler impelled the Court decisively to the right; and the subsequent addition of Stone was not enough to change the balance.

The Hughes Court

What is more, Herbert Hoover, a Republican president with considerably more liberal and humanitarian impulses than either of his two immediate predecessors, can hardly be blamed for what happened during the thirties. Of course Smith could have done better, in the sense of making more liberal appointments than Hoover did; but first he had to win the election. Hoover's first appointment was Hughes to replace Taft; and Hughes's previous record as an associate justice whom Taft had appointed to the early White Court, for which Hughes and Holmes formed the left wing, was clearly liberal for that day, on both economic and civil liberties issues and more so than was Holmes's own record voting in the same cases. Even such a libertarian critic of the Court as Fred Rodell has characterized Hughes's service as an associate justice as "six stunningly liberal years." [24] Hoover's second choice for the Court, in place of Sanford (who had died on the same day as Taft) was John J. Parker, a North Carolina lily-white Republican who was opposed by Senate liberals as being antilabor and anti-Negro, and who by a 41–39 margin became the first presidential nominee to the Court to be rejected in this century—I say "first" because I believe that Fortas's nomination to the chief justiceship, although technically a case of withdrawal that did not come to a vote, is functionally the second such instance. As John Frank has pointed out, labor and the NAACP picked a poor test case to demonstrate their veto power, judging by Parker's subsequent performance as the presiding judge of the Fourth Circuit United States Court of Appeals until his death in 1958, a role in which Parker built a record opposite to that of Hutcheson in the Fifth Circuit, standing behind the New Deal and even anticipating the Supreme Court in some aspects of racial segregation policy.[25] Not only labor and Negroes, but the country generally, might have been much better off if Parker, rather than Owen Roberts, had been voting in the policy decisions of the Hughes Court.[26] Roberts, whom Hoover picked as a noncontroversial substitute for Parker, was a Philadelphia corporation lawyer, a political associate of conservative Republican Senator George Wharton Pepper, and the prosecutor of the Teapot Dome scandals of the Harding administration.

Two years later, when Holmes retired, Hoover was induced to appoint in his place Benjamin N. Cardozo, a liberal, scholarly Democrat and Jew who was chief judge of the New York Court of Appeals. Cardozo soon established his position as that of the most liberal member of the Hughes Court, in close association with Stone and Brandeis. Neither Hughes nor Roberts developed a consistent affiliation with either the three-justice liberal or the four-justice conservative bloc during the early years of the Hughes Court. So the net effect of Hoover's three appointments was to substitute one moderate conservative for another (Roberts for Sanford), one relatively extreme (for his day) liberal for a much less dedicated one (Cardozo for Holmes), and one moderate for a conservative (Hughes for Taft); clearly the result was more liberal than the *status quo ante* had been. As in so many other aspects of his administration, Hoover had the misfortune to be the wrong man in the wrong place at the wrong time. It was not that most of the appointments that he made to the Supreme Court, including the one that he tried to make but failed, were not of eminently well politically qualified men and in what was for the time the correct (i.e., left-of-center) ideological direction; but it was too little, and too late, to compensate for the increasing chasm between the policy preferences of the four-man residual faction, who had helped to dominate the choices of the Taft Court, and the mood of the national electorate that had swept Franklin Roosevelt into office. As we have seen, there were several possible alternatives that did not materialize: Clarke could have provided one, and Parker another. But it was not simply a question of the ideological schism within the Court; Roosevelt was correct in attacking the entire group of Nine Old Men, including Brandeis and Cardozo and Stone. He was not correct from a tactical point of view, of course, but he was correct in the sense that there was a gap between the Wilsonian-Progressive type of liberalism represented by the liberal bloc of the Hughes Court, and what were for that time the more radical concepts of economic and social reform that formed the core of the more permanent program of the New Deal that began to evolve by the mid-thirties. Even the most liberal member of the Hughes Court, that is to say, was too conservative to experience other than cognitive dissonance between his own personal beliefs and the policies that Roosevelt wanted the Court to uphold.

There was, moreover, another and quite different respect in which the older liberalism and conservatism, of the period prior to 1937 that we have been considering thus far, differ from this ideology in the post-1937 period. The structure of liberal and conservative policy differences was so sharply delineated during the 1935 term, for example, that if one arranges all of the thirty-six split decisions for that term, in the sequence (ranging from most liberal to most conservative) Cardozo-Stone-Brandeis-Hughes-Roberts-Van Devanter-Sutherland-Butler-McReynolds, there are only five in-consistent votes altogether, and thirty-two of the thirty-six decisions scale perfectly, so that the ratio of consistent to total votes is above .98. (Furthermore, when this same scale is used to analyze the thirty-five decisions of the following 1936 term, the finding is equivalent, with a consistency ratio of .97.)[27] One must conclude, therefore, that during both the term before and the term of the Court-packing episode, both before and after the president's attack on the Court, there were highly consistent differences in the de-grees of liberalism, not only among the three blocs of liberal, moderate, and conservative justices, but also *within* each bloc and within the entire group of all three blocs. Moreover, these differences extended across the board to cover all issues that the Court decided during these two terms. From the be-ginning of the Taft Court until the Roosevelt Court, this single ideological dimension of liberalism/conservatism can account for all but a very small amount of the variance in the voting behavior of the justices. Such an observation can be explained, in part, by the small proportion of civil liberties cases decided before 1937, by which I mean explicitly that the civil liberties sample was so small that it may not ade-quately have revealed whatever imbalance there may have been, in the relative degrees of liberalism or conservatism of the individual justices, toward these two different kinds of policy question—and I am confident that this explanation would hold for Stone, for example. And it was probably also true—although this may well be merely an alternative way to state the same point—that the absolute differences be-tween the liberals and the conservatives of the pre-1937 Court were so much greater than the differences that ob-tained thereafter that the Court did not schedule for consideration the more moderate types of issues that might better have broken up the seeming ideological monolithicity of the two blocs: as long, that is to say, as the cases were selected to present extreme questions, they provoked correspondingly extreme answers, to some extent in both directions but mostly slanted conservatively.

I should like to illustrate what I mean by "the small amount of variance in the voting behavior of the justices," that remains unexplained by the ideological scale. Of course, every one of these men had certain idiosyncrasies; and to me, the wonder is not that they did have, but rather that they show up so slightly in their conjoint performance together. Taft's solicitude for kiddies and the weaker sex, previously noted, is one example; another is provided by McReynolds. A standard constitutional history speaks of "the surprising concurrence of six other justices, including the conservative McReynolds, in the Holmes argument" upholding the federal government's use of a treaty with Canada as the basis for a program of wild life conservation for migratory game birds, in *Missouri v. Holland*.[28] "The decision," remark the learned authors, "seemed to open a serious breach in the limited character of federal sovereignty."[29] McReynolds's support of the Migratory Bird Act of 1918 is less surprising, perhaps, when one considers that he was an inveterate duck hunter, who felt quite free to absent himself from Washington, from time to time and with or without prior notice to Taft, for a few autumnal days in the marshes of Chesapeake Bay;[30] and a similar explanation doubtless applies to Mac's solitary (and economically quite liberal!) dissent from the opening decision of the 1928 term, which found his colleagues challenging Louisiana's control over the taking of shrimp from the state's marshes: McReynolds's opinion starts right in by invoking precedents that concerned "woodcock, ruffled grouse, and quail." Or we might consider

Butler's dissenting votes, without opinion, against what were otherwise the Court's unanimous anti–civil liberties decisions in *Buck* v. *Bell*[31] and *Palko* v. *Connecticut*,[32] the former involving involuntary sexual sterilization, and the latter capital punishment notwithstanding a plea of double jeopardy. His strong Catholic ties[33] might well account for the first dissent, although not, it is true, the second. Moreover, Butler voted with the liberal bloc (of Brandeis, Holmes, and Stone) and even wrote a dissenting opinion to protest the conservative outcome of *Olmstead* v. *United States*,[34] the Court's first wiretap case. Danelski has pointed out, furthermore, that "Butler was not only sensitive to claims of procedural due process; his record indicates he was the Court's champion of those claims from 1923 to 1939. In the sixteen non-unanimous criminal cases involving issues of due process decided during that period, Butler voted for the defendant 75 percent of the time, compared with the majority's . . . 44 percent. . . . The fact that Butler dissented in favor of due-process claims in eight of those cases is a measure of the intensity of his feeling on such issues, for he abhorred the expression of dissent and frequently acquiesced in silence to decisions he voted against in conference. . . . Butler's record in cases involving substantive issues of freedom, however, was a curious reversal of his due-process record. In the fourteen non-unanimous cases that presented substantive issues of freedom such as freedom of speech or conscience, he voted for the individual only 29 per cent of the time, compared with the majority's . . . 50 per cent." [35] So except for the fair procedure component of civil liberties, Butler voted in accord with his conservative position on the more general ideological scale; and so far as I am aware, the reason for Butler's exceptionally and atypically libertarian sympathy for fair procedure remains unexplained.[36]

THE CONSTITUTIONAL POLITY

The Roosevelt Court

Chief Justice Hughes did not retire until four years later at the end of the 1940 term, but the successive appointments of Black and five other men of the president's choice left only Stone, Hughes himself, and Roberts (of the 1936 term Court) by the spring of 1941. This meant that the former conservative bloc was completely gone by then, and probably gone forever in the sense that it seems highly improbable that circumstances will arise in which it would be possible for the American political system to make available persons who represent the standpoint toward economic and social policy that was dominant in the Supreme Court until the spring of 1937. Every one of Roosevelt's appointees represented a point of view more liberal than that of Hughes or Roberts, so it is not surprising that the two center justices, who represented a middle-of-the-road position even in the first half of the 1936 term, now found themselves, just a little over four years later, on the right wing of the Court. Roberts remained in the end-man position for another four years as the most conservative member of the Roosevelt Court;[37] and when he retired in 1945, both the older conservatism typified by Taft, and the older moderation represented by Roberts himself, had disappeared. What remained were divisions within a point of view that had been represented, in the early Taft Court, primarily by John Clarke, and to a lesser extent by Louis Brandeis and Wendell Holmes, and to which Stone and Cardozo subsequently had made contributions.

So one respect in which the Roosevelt (and subsequent) Courts differed from their pre-1937 predecessors is that they occupied substantially nonoverlapping, and more liberal, segments of the ideological continuum than did the Taft or

98

Hughes Courts. Another difference, and an equally important one, is that a single dimension no longer suffices to distinguish the important differences among the justices comprising the Roosevelt, the Vinson, or the Warren Courts. Once civil liberties cases began to preempt an increasing share of the Court's time and attention, as they did after 1937, and as they had come so conspicuously to do during the sixties under the Warren Court, then it is no longer adequate to speak simply of liberals and conservatives. I shall refer henceforth, therefore, to economic liberals and economic conservatives, and to political liberals and political conservatives, although I feel impelled to confess that even the use of two dimensions tends to oversimplify the Warren Court period, and a better job could be done with a threefold analytical framework. The data to support such a task are not yet available, however; and much work needs to be done, in revising and recasting the attitudinal research of judicial behavioralists during the past decade, before such a more sophisticated analysis will be possible.

The reason why at least two scales are needed to discuss differences among the post-1937 judges is not difficult to apprehend. Some justices, when confronted with samples of cases that constitute a broad array of issues relating to civil liberties policy, as well as an equivalent array relating to economic policy, give equally sympathetic support (or else fail to do so) both within and between the two policy fields: such persons are consistent liberals (or conservatives, as the case may be). But some other justices (as it happened in fact, a minority) may be sympathetic to civil liberties claims but yet may be economically conservative, or vice versa; and it is because of them that the two dimensions are needed in order to discuss their behavior. There is also a third possibility: that a judge may be consistent in his posture *between* the two dimensions (e.g., he votes mostly

as either a liberal or a conservative on both political and economic issues), but inconsistent *within* (that is, between the subcomponents of) one (or conceivably, both) of them (e.g., he is pro privacy but anti fair procedure). We should have to describe such a person as having relatively low communality with the cognitive framework shared by the rest of the Court; and I have no doubt but that it is not uncommon to find such deviant cases in many empirical samples of respondents—including, to use an example with which I have some detailed familiarity, samples consisting of professors of constitutional law and the judicial process.[38] But academicians do not have to go through the same kind of recruitment process as do Supreme Court justices; and my hypothesis about this matter is that persons with an idiosyncratic (that is, queer, atypical) point of view are not considered available for appointment to the Court. The debate among the justices, that is to say, takes place within relatively narrow (as well as highly stylized and quite conventional) limits. So we have only one such deviant case to consider, in our analysis of the post-1937 Supreme Court, and even in this single instance, it took a quarter of a century on the Court for the inconsistency to exceed what I previously have referred to as the normal range of human idiosyncrasy (as exemplified by Taft's soft spot or McReynold's ducks) so that one naturally begins to suspect that the problem, to which we shall turn in more detail presently, has much in common with such other manifestations of aging as, say, Henry Baldwin's derangement, Robert Grier's sleeping at the bench (after he had been carried to it), Henry Brown's blindness, or Nathan Clifford's senility.[39]

F.D.R.'s appointments were mostly New Deal Democrats, as one would have expected. First came Hugo Black, the Southern poor-white Ku Klux Klan member, son of a Confederate veteran, and militant social and economic liberal

United States senator. The immediate effect of Black's appointment in the summer of 1937 was to assure that there would be no backsliding from the policy changes that had taken place during the spring, by establishing a majority bloc of the left-center which included all except the three remaining conservatives. During the next two years, Roosevelt added Stanley Reed, a Kentucky Democrat and government lawyer who as solicitor general had argued many of the major New Deal cases; Felix Frankfurter, a Harvard professor of constitutional and administrative law who professed to be "Independent" in his partisan attachments—after all, Holmes and Brandeis, his two intellectual idols, both were Republicans—but who long had been identified with causes, both economic and civil libertarian, that were liberal in terms of the pre-1937 meaning of that concept; and William Douglas, a Yale professor of tax law and Democrat who had served in the New Deal as chairman of the Securities and Exchange Commission. The effect of these three appointments was less than one might suppose, because the three justices replaced were Cardozo, Brandeis, and Sutherland—two liberals and one conservative—so that the net result was to establish a new bloc consisting of the four modern liberals (Black, Douglas, Frankfurter, and Reed), with Stone, Hughes, and Roberts arrayed (and in that order) in the middle, leaving only Butler and McReynolds as the surviving right-wing conservatives. The substitution of Frank Murphy, a former Michigan Democratic governor of the Philippines, for Pierce Butler (who was also, it will be recalled, a midwestern Democrat and Roman Catholic), was a more radical change, making possible for the next two terms (1939 and 1940) a majority bloc of the five new Roosevelt appointees plus Stone, with Murphy fitting in between Douglas and Frankfurter. The effect was to push Hughes and Roberts into a right-wing affiliation with

McReynolds: Hughes, for example, had agreed with Mc-Reynolds in only 29 per cent of the split decisions of the 1936 term, according to Pritchett's data, but they were in agreement 94 per cent of the time in their final (the 1940) term.[40]

The reduction of the Hughes Court to Roberts entailed the consequence, however, that the center of debate within the Court had to shift, away from the differences between the Roosevelt and the other justices, to the differences *among* the Roosevelt appointees. This began in the 1941 term. Stone had been promoted by Roosevelt, as a gesture toward bipartisanship with American participation *de jure* in World War II imminent; and there has been much discussion of the relative merits of Stone and Hughes as presiding officers, the conventional view being that Hughes ran a tight ship and that Stone tolerated—indeed, encouraged—too much intra-Court democracy, debate, and dissent. I should hope to be the last to denigrate the possible relevance of sociopsychological explanations of the Court's decision-making processes, including those related to organization theories of group leadership; but it does seem to me that insufficient attention has been given to another obvious hypothesis, also drawn from sociopsychological theory, which emphasizes the group social structure more than the processes of leadership. With Hughes and McReynolds gone, the eight Roosevelt appointees (now including Stone) could hardly pass the time demonstrating their capacity to outvote Roberts; and so, having gotten rid of the former opposition over which their victory was by then substantially complete, they began to explore more carefully the differences among themselves. This inquiry quickly revealed important differences, on both economic and civil liberties issues, between a new and more extreme liberal bloc, and the remainder of the Roosevelt justices, just as there remained until his retirement at the end of the war important differences of degree between the moderate liberalism of these other Roosevelt appointees and the conservatism of Roberts. Note that I am *not* suggesting that Roberts, who was the median justice in the 1936 term, had "grown more conservative" during the ensuing decade; it is rather my explicit thesis that Roberts probably was pulled somewhat more in the *liberal* direction because of the social influences emanating from the new group of Roosevelt justices, to which he was exposed. But the issues they brought before the Court for him to decide were considerably more extreme in their claims, and therefore required a greater degree of liberalism to support them, than those that had confronted the Hughes Court; and so, in responding to such more extreme issues and in relation to a group of men who were, without much exception (see below), more sympathetic than he to upholding the new extreme claims of liberalism, Roberts could not appear other than as he did—relatively, the most conservative member of the Roosevelt Court during the period of Stone's chief justiceship.

For only a single term, Roosevelt had replaced McReynolds with James Byrnes, a South Carolina Democrat who had been (like Black) a pillar of the New Deal in the United States Senate (and, subsequently, a segregationist governor); Byrnes, in turn, was replaced by Wiley Rutledge, a former University of Iowa law school dean and Democrat, who had served briefly during the war as a federal circuit judge on the Court of Appeals of the District of Columbia.

The political liberalism scale for the Roosevelt Court was: Murphy, Rutledge, Black, and Douglas, followed by Stone, Frankfurter, Jackson, Reed, Byrnes, and Roberts. The economic scale was: Black, Douglas, Murphy, and Rutledge, and then Reed, Byrnes, Frankfurter, Jackson, Stone, and Roberts. The group whom Pritchett has called the "Libertarian Four" are positive on both scales, and they are the only ones who have positive records of support on either scale; and we can appropriately designate them as "liberals." Similarly, during this period, Frankfurter and Jackson were moderately negative on both scales,[41] and we can refer to them as moderate conservatives; while Roberts, who was last on both scales, was the Roosevelt Court's conservative. For the other three justices, however, there are more important differences in their rankings on the two scales. Stone was more sympathetic to political than to economic liberalism, voting as a moderate on civil liberties and a conservative on economic issues. Reed and Byrnes, on the other hand, were moderates on the economic scale and conservatives on civil liberties. (And it bears repeating, at this point, that I am referring to relative differences within the new field in which debate was then taking place on the Roosevelt Court, a field that was in its own range strictly "liberal" in comparison with the scope of issues that had been considered by the pre-1937 Court.)

The effect of the Rutledge appointment in 1943, giving the Roosevelt Court a strong (albeit still a minority) bloc of four, was mitigated by the war milieu, which produced such results as the unanimous Roosevelt Court, including all four liberals, upholding the racist military policy of the West Coast curfew for Japanese-American citizens; and with Murphy the only liberal to protest the subsequent decision justifying the evacuation program, which found Black mouthing such pointless platitudes as that "hardships are part of war, and war is an aggregation of hardships." [42] Consequently, most of the wartime support for civil liberties was given to relatively harmless defendants, such as Jehovah's Witnesses whose complaints were levied against local government policies for civilians rather than against the national war effort.

CONSTITUTIONAL POLITICS

The Vinson Court

The 1945 term was transitional between the Roosevelt and Truman Courts. Harold Burton, a Republican United States senator from Ohio and a Truman crony, replaced Roberts at the beginning of the term; and Burton also took Roberts's place as the most conservative member of the Court. However, Jackson's absence, throughout the term whilst he was off in Nuremberg bringing justice to the vanquished, left the Court short handed. One might have thought that the result would have been a Court deadlocked between the four liberals and the other four; but in the event, as Pritchett's data show,[43] this was the most homogeneous Court, with the least range of disagreement, of any since 1930, for the apparent reason that the substitution of a freshman justice for the Court's senior associate justice had a moderating effect upon the group, which was reinforced by the absence of Jackson (and his feuds with both Murphy and Black). And there were very few civil liberty decisions this term; instead, there was an unusually high proportion of taxation and other fiscal claims, and of questions of the respective scope of competence of judges and administrators —administrative law buffs will recall that the Federal Administrative Procedure Act was under consideration at this time, and was enacted the following year. And actually, there was only a seven-man Court for what was decisionally the last third of the term, because of Stone's death in April.

The appointment of Fred Vinson as chief justice, two months later, changed the balance of the Court. And Jackson returned in the fall, with all the exacerbation of personal relationships consequent to his public attack, in June, upon Hugo Black—Jackson had charged Black with lobbying with Truman to prevent his own (Jackson's) promotion in accordance with Roosevelt's promise, thus making possible the selection of Vinson. The Vinson Court then included four liberals, of whom two (Douglas and Black) were relatively most sympathetic to economic claims and the other two (Murphy and Rutledge) were more sympathetic to civil liberties—indeed, they were the most pro–civil liberties justices ever to have served on the Court, before or since. Frankfurter and Jackson, now that Stone was gone, became the ones to whom the four liberals had to turn in order to construct a pro–civil liberties majority, and thenceforth both Frankfurter and Jackson became the Vinson Court's middle on civil liberties issues, while remaining the right wing on economic issues. The two Truman appointees, Vinson and Burton, joined with Reed to form the Court's middle on economic issues, while voting conservatively on civil liberties —the aggregated votes of all three of them upheld 28 per cent of claims to economic liberalism, but only 10 per cent of the civil liberties claims, during the 1946 to 1948 terms. Vinson, in his first term on the Court, voted against every one of the score of civil liberties claims presented, while Burton and Reed upheld only two each. As we already have noted, the wartime milieu had repressed what might otherwise have become a much more pro–civil liberties policy for the Court, during the three years after the appointment of Rutledge and before the death of Stone; and the war docket continued to affect the Court during the 1946 term, as indicated by both the small number of civil liberties claims even considered, and of those the very low proportion that were upheld. During the 1946 term, the four liberals voted together in support of nine civil liberties claims, and they were able to attract a fifth vote, from among their five colleagues, in only two such instances, so that the proportion of pro cases was only 22 per cent. But the next two terms showed promise of the Court undertaking then to reconsider the civil liberties sector, just as it had reformulated its conservative economic policies in a much more liberal direction before the war. The volume of civil liberties cases doubled, and the proportion upheld more than quadrupled, with the four liberals now attracting support—from precisely the same group of colleagues as during the 1946 term—in 63 per cent of the thirty-five instances in which they themselves voted as a bloc in support of political liberalism. This seemingly important development was cut off, shortly and sharply, by the deaths of the two principal proponents of civil libertarianism, Murphy and Rutledge, at the end of the 1948 term.

In their place Harry Truman put Tom Clark, a Texas Democrat and former Dallas prosecutor who had risen (like Robert Jackson, at an earlier time) through the legal ranks of the federal Department of Justice; and Sherman Minton, an Indiana Democrat who had been a Senate crony of Truman, the Democratic whip of the Senate during the New Deal, and (after being defeated for reelection) a federal court of appeals judge. But one thing should be said in Truman's behalf: while he single-mindedly packed the Court with personal patronage, he unwittingly succeeded, far better than did his more ideologically motivated immediate predecessor or successor in the presidency, in appointing men who consistently, all of them, were chips off the old block. In Truman's case, this meant being moderately conservative in their support of economic claims, and strongly conservative in regard to civil liberties. So the structure of the latter period of the Vinson Court was: only two liberals, Black and Douglas; two who were moderates in their support of civil liberties, but economic conservatives, Frankfurter and Jackson; and a new majority which was relatively moderate in regard to economic issues but conservative on civil liberties—Vinson, Reed, Burton, Clark, and Minton.

Clearly such a group was stacked—and by Truman—in favor of maintaining the status quo on economic policy, and in favor of repudiating the civil libertarian changes that had begun in the two preceding years. Both of these trends in fact occurred; and both were accentuated by two chance occurrences: Douglas missed all except the very end of the 1949 term, due to an injury; and it was during this same period that Joseph McCarthy came to symbolize the inauguration of a period of several years of repression of civil liberties, throughout the country. As a consequence, the last four years of the Vinson Court were even more reactionary than might have been the case, had it not been for these— from the Court's point of view—fortuitous reinforcements.

The Early Warren Court—1953–1962

The selection of Earl Warren as Vinson's successor, at the beginning of the 1953 term, has proved to be probably the most important thing that Dwight Eisenhower did as president—and I do not intend that remark to be taken, as I guess well it might without this caveat, as damnation by faint praise. Warren's first two terms were a learning experience for him, and it was not until the 1955 term that Warren began to play the characteristic policy role that he maintained thereafter. In the meantime, three events of relevance for us occurred. McCarthy was censured and with his departure from the national scene went one highly negative, if indirect, constraint upon the Court's range of possibilities for liberalizing its policy toward civil liberties. Jackson died, to be replaced by John Marshall Harlan, the namesake of the Court's only civil libertarian prior to the appointment of Brandeis. Apart from the irony of having the name of the man who wrote one of the truly great pieces

of prophetic liberal rhetoric in American political history—
the solitary dissent in *Plessy* v. *Ferguson*—passed on to a
grandson who is now the Warren Court's anchorman (or
next to him) on issues of both civil liberties and economic
liberalism, Harlan was as close a fit as a replacement for
Bob Jackson, even down to the details of minor and sub-
component issues, as it is possible to get when one individual
takes over another's place and role. Harlan junior was a
Wall Street corporation lawyer and a Dewey Republican.
The third event concerns Clark, who had voted hand-in-
glove with Warren on civil liberties during the 1953 and
1954 terms, but who then reverted to his former position
when the new chief kept on moving too far, and too fast,
to the left. The 1955 term was transitional, with Warren
continuing his shift to assume a position of affirmative support immediately behind Douglas and Black, while Clark
began to retreat, from his tie with Warren in the middle of
the Court and support of slightly over half of the civil
liberties claims during the 1954 term, to the position of bot-
tom rank on civil liberties support which he assumed in
the 1956 term and retained, or shared with Harlan, for his
remaining ten years on the Court. So in 1955 the Warren
Court was perfectly balanced on civil liberties with three
liberals (Douglas, Black, and Warren); three moderates
(Frankfurter, Clark, and Harlan); and three conservatives
(Burton, Minton, and Reed). The structure was more favorable toward economic liberalism, with four liberals (Douglas, Black, Warren, and Clark); three moderates (Reed,
Minton, and Burton); and two conservatives (Frankfurter
and Harlan). The effect of the difference in having only
three instead of four supporters of an issue, and of having
three instead of two opponents, is shown by the differences,
both quantitative and qualitative, in the outcomes: only 41
per cent of twenty-two civil liberties claims were upheld,

but 80 per cent of thirty-nine economic claims—twice as high a rate for almost twice as many cases—were upheld in the 1955 term.

It was in the following term that the Warren Court assumed the structure that was to characterize it for the remainder of the decade. Minton retired at the beginning, and Reed in the middle, of the 1956 term. Eisenhower replaced Minton with William Brennan, a New Jersey Democrat and state supreme court judge who had been raised in a working-class immigrant home, and who was selected to provide the Roman Catholic representation that had been missing since Murphy's demise because Truman, with characteristic broad-mindedness, felt that appointments to the Supreme Court ought to be based strictly on merit, and without regard to race, creed, or color. (One is reminded of the old Henry Ford gag about the Model T: "Paint it any color you like, just so long as it's black!") Clearly, this was Eisenhower's second big mistake in staffing the Supreme Court; not as bad an error as he made with Warren, but still an important one, because Brennan immediately assumed a position as the Court's fourth-ranking liberal, on both major issues, immediately behind Warren. Although Brennan has consistently given slightly less support to either civil liberties or economic claims than has Warren, Brennan has upheld preponderant majorities of claims on both issues in every one of his dozen terms on the Court. Eisenhower's next choice turned out to be a safer bet. Charles Whittaker, a Missouri farm boy and a Republican who had become a highly successful corporation lawyer, immediately staked out the most economically conservative position as his own, although on civil liberties, he voted as a moderate conservative, like Frankfurter and Harlan.

The result of these changes, in both the external and the internal environments of the Court, was soon reflected in significant developments in the Court's policy outputs. Because Whittaker was more, and Brennan was considerably more, sympathetic to civil liberties than either Minton or Reed, there was a sharp increase both in the number and in the proportion of favorable civil liberties decisions. Many of these were the first decisions that the Court had ever made to uphold the rights of political freedom and of privacy of Communists and fellow travelers before congressional and state legislative committees, and it was really the first time in our national history that the Supreme Court had begun to take seriously the First Amendment, and to demand that others do so, too. It was no coincidence that what we might call this civil liberties backlash should have coincided, as it did, with the interment of McCarthyism (and of McCarthy too, although the man himself had really become irrelevant by then). Many conservatives in Congress were, of course, outraged to think that anybody, and least of all the Supreme Court, should uphold the First Amendment as a norm for social action; and so it was that, after a lapse of twenty years, the Supreme Court again came under attack, but now for the opposite reason: because the Court had become too liberal and was interfering with the political policies of the federal and state governments. I shall discuss this episode in greater detail in the next chapter; but one or two points must be made now. It is perfectly clear that the votes that made possible the libertarian resurgence of 1956 and 1957 were those of Frankfurter and Harlan because the four liberals could not decide cases favorably without a fifth vote. In particular, it was Felix Frankfurter who supplied that vote in these terms.[44] It is also perfectly clear what happened in response to the Jenner and Mallory bills and other Court-curbing legislation that was building up to a vote during the 1958 term: Frankfurter switched. The Court's lifelong student, and the apologist for Roberts's switch in 1937, had learned his lessons well;[45] and he took Harlan with him, just as Hughes had taken Roberts with him a generation earlier. On issues such as *Watkins/Barenblatt* and *Sweezy/Uphaus* that were substantially equivalent (except for the congressional reaction that intervened between these pairs of cases), the dimensions of Frankfurter's switch are perhaps best illustrated by noting that in both the 1956 and 1957 terms, Frankfurter voted fifth, and Clark ninth, on civil liberties issues, with Frankfurter voting to uphold twenty-three of forty-four and twenty-eight of fifty-five, a majority in each of the two terms, for a rate of 52 per cent, while Clark upheld four of forty-four and then only two of fifty-six, for an average of 6 per cent. In the 1958 term, however, Frankfurter upheld four of twenty-seven (15 per cent) and Clark two of twenty-nine (7 per cent). Stated slightly differently, Frankfurter agreed with Clark only half of the time in the 1956 and 1957 terms, while in 1958 they were in agreement in 85 per cent of the civil liberties decisions, voting alike in twenty-three of twenty-seven decisions.

History did not repeat itself; the moving finger writes, and having writ, moves on. But the same kind of judicial tactic resulted, for the second time, in a deflection of the move to reorganize the Court by legislation. There, however, the similarity ends. The 1937 change was enduring, in the sense that the redirection of trends, stemming from that episode, has continued as a long range development up to the present day. This happened because, as we have seen, the Hughberts switch (as I have sometimes called it, with apologies to a former graduate student of mine, Peter Meloney, who named the game and then escaped from political science to philosophy) was reinforced by personnel changes in the same direction as the switch. With Frankfurter's switch, the opposite has happened.

Even the personnel change that took place at the beginning of the 1958 term, when Burton was replaced by Potter Stewart, an Ohio Republican and corporation lawyer whose father was a state supreme court justice, worked against Frankfurter's purposes, because Stewart was a civil liberties moderate and economic conservative, unlike Burton who had been a civil liberties conservative and economic moderate. Stewart remained the center of the Court on civil liberties issues for the next four terms, as evidenced by the fact that he voted in the majority in all except 15 of 148 civil liberties decisions. Hence Frankfurter's switch was important primarily in the withholding of his own support, although apparently he was influential in inducing Harlan and Whittaker to withhold theirs too—and Clark needed no persuasion. But this meant that it was Stewart, the Court's freshman justice, and not Frankfurter, who could determine most of the time which way the Court's civil liberties decisions would go. So in this respect the parallel with 1937 breaks down. If Burton had chosen, as so many of his predecessors had done, to stick it out on the Court for the next several years instead of going into retirement, Frankfurter would have benefited in two ways: (1) he could have avoided the dozen or so decisions that Stewart gave to the liberals; and (2) he, Frankfurter, could personally have filled the role of the strategically important center justice on this issue, instead of Stewart's doing so, because Burton almost certainly would have continued to choose to vote (like Clark) more conservatively than Frankfurter and Harlan and Whittaker.

But as it was, Frankfurter's last five years on the Court were dedicated to opposing the Warren Court's resumption of a policy of greater civil libertarianism. For a much longer time, however, he had been conservative on certain civil liberties issues, such as the right to privacy against state officials;[46] and in these respects his customary conservatism became more extreme. Just a year before his enforced retirement, for instance, Frankfurter was the Court's only dissenter against a decision that privacy had been invaded when "13 Chicago police officers broke into petitioner's home in the early morning, routed them [that is, six black children, and their father and mother] from bed, made them stand naked in the living room, and ransacked every room, emptying drawers and ripping mattress covers," with neither a search nor an arrest warrant. Frankfurter's dissent begins: "Abstractly stated, this case concerns a matter of statutory construction." And then he even has the poor grace—and no one has ever accused him of insensitivity to verbal nuances —to indulge himself in what, under the circumstances, can only be described as a very bad pun, because the sentence that follows begins: "So stated, the problem before the Court is denuded"—denuded!—"of illuminating concreteness and thereby of its far-reaching significance"—and again, I must interject: one might expect a phrase such as "for human dignity" or "for civil liberty" to follow; but do you know what does? For Frankfurter, the significance is "for our federal system." [47] As Cliff Grant summed it up, in a poignant but perceptive memoir of the progenitor of what he calls *Frankfurterweise,*

> It has been said of Holmes that he survived into his own generation. It may yet be written of Frankfurter that he was appointed as his was passing into history. He came to the Court beautifully equipped to carry on the Holmes-Brandeis opposition to judicial activism in the economic field. In twenty-three years on the bench he had occasion to write just one such opinion. He came totally ill-equipped, emotionally as well as from his sense of values, to meet the challenge of a new era. Although he came from Vienna rather than from Paris, in a way his history is so French. For France, it will be re-

called, on the eve of World War II was so beautifully
prepared for World War I.[48]

The Later Warren Court—1962–1969

The congressional campaign to curb the Court was over
by 1960; and the election of John F. Kennedy foreclosed
any possibility there might have been of backing up Frankfurter's switch with some appropriately conservative Nixon
appointments. And unlike F.D.R., who had to wait five
years and launch a major political assault before he could
make an appointment to the Court, Kennedy had two at his
disposal in his second year. Whittaker announced his retirement on April 1, 1962, and only a week or so later Frankfurter was forced by a heart attack to withdraw from further
participation, although his formal retirement did not come
until the end of August. The immediate consequence of
the removal of Frankfurter and Whittaker was that, even
though they had taken part in about a third of the decisions
for the term, the proportion of pro–civil liberties decisions
jumped from less than half to almost three-fourths. There
was little effect upon economic decisions which had been
averaging about 70 per cent pro–economic liberalism in recent terms, even with both Frankfurter and Whittaker participating. The political liberalism scale for the seven continuing justices was, at this time, Douglas, Black, Warren,
Brennan, Stewart, Harlan, and Clark; and the economic
liberalism scale was the same except that on it Clark ranked
between Brennan and Stewart.

The 1961 term marks the end of the initial period of the
Warren Court, one in which, as we have seen, the Court
continued its generally liberal posture on economic issues,
and moved strongly forward but then retreated in its development of a line on civil liberties. I think that it is perfectly

clear that what course the Court might have followed in the sixties, in regard to either issue, remained open in the spring of 1962, depending upon what kind of New Frontiersmen Kennedy should select. As it turned out, of course, these were to be his only chances to make appointments to the Supreme Court.

Byron "Whizzer" White was a Democrat, former All-American, and a Rhodes scholar who had been Vinson's law clerk, and who in the role of deputy attorney general had dispensed judicial patronage for the Kennedy administration.[49] White has proved to be no great liberal, however. Instead, he has played the role of the consistent moderate conservative, deviating very little from Whittaker's overall position on civil liberties, although he has been substantially less conservative on economic issues than was Whittaker. Since he joined the Court almost seven years ago, White has continued to rank between fifth and eighth in his support of both issues. He has tended to be particularly sympathetic to union claims, but less liberal than Stewart on questions of racial equality and political freedom.

Kennedy's other appointment, to replace Frankfurter, was Arthur Goldberg, a labor lawyer and Democrat from Chicago, an immigrant's son and a Jew, who proved during his brief time on the Court to be moderately sympathetic to civil liberties, and about the same as White toward economic claims. So the upshot was that the New Frontier's contribution to the Supreme Court was one tepid conservative, and an individualistic political liberal who gave only lukewarm support to economic liberalism and who soon resigned from his mundane tasks on the Court to replace Stevenson at the United Nations.

In practice and in context, however, the effect of the two Kennedy appointees, upon the Warren Court's civil liberty policies, was by no means unimportant. The two assumed a position between Brennan and Stewart, in their support of civil liberties, with Goldberg fifth and White sixth in rank order; and Goldberg did provide the fifth reliable liberal vote in favor of civil liberties for the first time in our political history. The new Warren majority began at once to accelerate the nationalization of the rights of fair procedure and of privacy, and to uphold political freedom against the national government to an extent that no Court ever had done before.

When Goldberg resigned in 1965, Johnson replaced him with Abe Fortas, a Democrat and Jew and senior partner of an unusually successful Washington law firm, who as counsel donating his services had helped to persuade the Warren Court to make many of its recent precedents expanding the rights of indigent criminal defendants.[50] Fortas soon became second only to Douglas, in his overall support of civil liberties, although with some variations (such as his relatively lower support for fair procedure); and in regard to economic claims, he took about the same position as White—slightly more liberal than Black, that is—and like Goldberg and White, his support for union claims was somewhat greater than his support for government regulation of business. Johnson's other appointment was to replace Tom Clark with Thurgood Marshall, a Democrat, the extraordinarily successful chief counsel for the NAACP who had helped to persuade the Court to accept most of the decisions that have come to make up the Warren Court's liberal policy on racial equality, and—it hardly needs to be repeated— the first Negro to be appointed to the Supreme Court. In his first two terms Marshall was no militant, voting dead center behind Brennan and Warren in the fifth position, on both civil liberties and economic claims. But both Johnson appointees proved to be more liberal than the men whom they replaced, so their effect has been to accentuate the civil libertarian development already under way. During Marshall's first term, the political liberalism scale was: Douglas, Fortas, Brennan, Warren, Marshall, Stewart, Black, White, and Harlan; but by the 1968 term, Black had become the Warren Court's anchorman on civil liberties, dissenting forty-one times (twenty-five of these alone) against the sixty-eight split pro–civil liberties decisions in which he participated: this was more than the combined total of such conservative dissents by his closest rivals (Harlan and Stewart); and with nineteen pro and forty-nine con votes in these decisions, Black was the *only* justice to vote mostly—to say nothing of predominantly—negatively on civil liberties issues during the final term of the Warren Court. The economic scale was: Douglas, Fortas Warren, Brennan, Marshall, White, Black, Stewart, and Harlan. Black's descent from second to ninth rank in support of the political variable, and his seventh rank on the economic scale, signify a change in his position on these issues opposite to the direction in which the Court itself had, as a group, been moving.

Clearly, Hugo Black, the senior associate (since 1946) who was the Court's first New Dealer, and who in the spring of 1969 was eighty-three years old and in his thirty-third year there, had begun to backslide, from what had been largely his public posture of staunch and outspoken and indeed activist support of both civil liberties and economic liberalism, for almost forty years—counting, as I do, his decade of service in the United States Senate as well as his tenure on the Supreme Court. The specific issue that marked the turning point for Black was that of the integration sit-in cases, which reached the Court for decision on the last day of the term in June 1964. Beginning right then, in a series of eight cases (covering various private facilities, ranging from Glen Echo Amusement Park in suburban

Washington to drugstore lunch counters), Black joined White and Harlan in dissent against decisions declaring that blacks have an equal right, under the Constitution, to share in accommodations open to the public.[51] And from then on, in regard to the issue of racial equality, Tom Clark provided the fifth liberal vote, followed by White, Stewart, Harlan, and Black, and *in that order*. During the next five terms, Hugo Black, long the hero of many of the Court's liberal commentators, played the role of the leader of the die-hard opposition to the Court's expansive policy of racial egalitarianism, often dissenting alone,[52] but usually in the company of Harlan, or Harlan and White, or occasionally Harlan and White and Stewart. Black was able to assign to himself the majority opinion on a few occasions, in one of which Clark joined the four conservatives to uphold the trespass conviction of a crowd of students who had demonstrated on a jailhouse lawn; similarly, at the end of that term in June 1967, Black assigned Stewart to write for the same majority upholding a civil rights injunction, by a local state court, to prohibit street parades without a permit.[53] There were six nonunanimous pro–racial equality decisions during the 1968 term, and Black dissented alone against all five of those in which he participated.

A second issue on which Black began, on the same day in June 1964, to stake out a position as the Court's most conservative member, is that of the right to privacy. There is, of course, little novelty in the suggestion that Black was not noted during his first fifteen years on the Court—prior, that is, to Warren—for his sympathy for Fourth Amendment claims, a matter that I had occasion to point out and document almost a decade ago;[54] but it is only during the past five years that Black has voted as the Court's arch conservative against any extension of the right to privacy, often alone, but otherwise with one or more of White, Stewart, and Harlan.[55] In the 1968 term, there were twenty-nine nonunanimous proprivacy decisions, and Black dissented against them all, including nineteen times in which he alone dissented.

A third civil liberties issue, in regard to which Black has voted much more conservatively, is fair procedure, regarding which Harlan and White voted most conservatively, followed closely by Black who was the *only* justice (other than Stewart) to dissent against fair procedure during the 1967 and 1968 terms. (Black continued, however, to be at the same time one of the two most frequent dissenters—the other was Douglas—against *anti*-fair procedure decisions.) In several instances Black dissented in the company of conservatives against other libertarian claims, such as civic equality[56] and the political freedom to picket and to demonstrate.[57] A good example of his alienation from both the Court and contemporary American society was his slashing dissent against the right of public school children to signify by the wearing of black armbands their political protest against the Vietnam War. Black thought that because of the majority's decision, many students "will be ready, able, and willing to defy their teachers on practically all orders. This is the more unfortunate," he said, "since groups of students all over the land are already running loose, conducting break-ins, sit-ins, lie-ins and smash-ins." [58] Only in regard to claims to such orthodox aspects of political freedom as freedom of speech (literally construed), and to the occasional claims to religious freedom or to voting equality, did Black stand fast in the liberal faith. Quite clearly, by any objective test his overall performance during the past several years has increasingly been much more that of a political conservative than of a political liberal.

What is perhaps even more surprising is his shift toward conservatism on economic issues, too. In split decisions

Black supported only a third (nine of twenty-six) of the labor claims during the 1965–1968 terms, including only one of six in the 1967 term.[59] Overall, he plummeted from first (1961–1964 terms) to seventh rank (1965–1968 terms) on the economic liberalism scale, with his proportion of pro (E^+) votes dropping from 88 per cent (1961–1964 terms) to 51 per cent (1967–1968 terms). Black's regression on economic policy, as well as his increasing conservatism on such civil liberties issues as privacy and fair procedure—for which the violence, if any, is visited upon the defendants by policemen, doctors, and other representatives of the forces of law and order—discredit, in my view, the explanation that (as Spaeth puts it) Black is reacting against the "extra-legal activities of civil rights demonstrators"[60] rather than against an excessive indulgence in "equality between the races," in the coddling of criminals,[61] and in freedom of communication. One opposed only to nonorthodox (viz., later than eighteenth century?) modes of political demonstrations, social dissent, and communication of radical ideas could limit his opposition to such matters; but Black does not do that. His reaction has become generic. No well-informed person today is unaware of the contagious spread of violence in the schools and of assault and looting in the streets, throughout much of the country; but riot and rebellion are poorly symbolized by fewer than half a dozen young blacks taking a ride on a merry-go-round in the District of Columbia region's largest and most popular amusement park, or by the wearing to school of armbands by three adolescents (of whom two, brother and sister, were children of a Methodist minister employed by the *Quakers*—a notoriously nonviolent group—and the other's mother was an officer in the Women's International League for Peace and Freedom). It was in the carousel case[62] that Black began to vote against claims to racial equality; and the armband decision[63] came almost five years later. Moreover, Black's votes in *Griffin* and in *Tinker* are typical of his behavior since June 1964, and only by casuistry can either of these cases, or the many others like them, be classified as examples of riotous radical protest. The latter type of issue has not yet even begun to be considered by the Supreme Court. It is, of course, possible that Black is right in voting conservatively to oppose free speech for high school students. It may, indeed, be the course of prudence to stamp out even the "single revolutionary spark [that] may kindle a fire that, smouldering for a time, may burst into a sweeping and destructive conflagration";[64] such was the Taft Court's response to political dissent. It may be that the Four Horsemen were right in resisting at all costs the threat to individualism presented by the New Deal. And it may be that the Supreme Court today should function, not as it has done under Warren, as an instrument to facilitate political, social, and economic change in the general direction of a broader sharing of values, but rather as the American House of Lords, a citadel of resistance to efforts (peaceful or otherwise) to bring about any redistribution in the established pattern of values. But one is at least entitled to doubt the wisdom of following the road to reaction. If one continues to embrace, not necessarily a radical point of view, but rather the liberal faith in efforts to accommodate and to compromise social conflict, as the most promising alternative to riotous and revolutionary solutions for such conflicts, then Black's present posture is a poor fit for the needs of our day; and it is to be regretted that a man who was for so long a leader in the manipulation of the judicial process to subserve democratic goals should have remained in office so long that he has become both an instrument and a spokesman against the very goals to which his public life had been dedicated.

Certainly Black is quite aware that, having been attacked by conservatives throughout most of his political career, he has in recent years become a target for critics from the left, both liberal and radical.[65] And I am quite aware of Black's own assertion that "in attempting to follow as best I can the Constitution as it appears to me to be written, and in attempting in all cases to resist reaching a result simply because I think it is desirable, I have been following a view of our government held by me at least as long as I have been a lawyer." [66] I realize also that the conventional view among academic observers is that Black has remained (as he himself says) a psychological constant in a socially dynamic world. A most perceptive student of the Court has confronted me with the question, which if not rhetorical is at least hyperbolic: "Could it be that this is not the time for the Court to legitimate every riot, trespass, inflammatory demand, threat of assassination, bombing and arson, and moralistic law-breaking gesture that comes along?" And he has added: "Perhaps Justice Black is the only one of the justices who has reacted, rightly or wrongly, to the real world of the sixties." Perhaps so; and I concede that it is both logically and empirically possible that everyone is out of step but Johnny. But in relation to the institution of which he is a part, as it has been composed for the past third of a century, it is highly inconsistent for Hugo Black to define his role as a relatively extreme conservative, instead of as a relatively extreme liberal, member of the Court. And I find it hard to accept the suggestion that Black is the only justice who understands what is going on in the world. Without calling the entire role of the Warren Court, I think it likely that Abe Fortas, Thurgood Marshall, William Douglas, and Earl Warren himself were as aware as Black of the violence, destruction, and social turmoil that are among the manifest consequences of radical drives for black power, student power, and peace power. They all knew when Washington was looted and burned, only a block from the Government Printing Office and not very far from the Marble Palace itself. But these same events pushed Douglas, with whom Black had been paired in voting on almost all issues for a quarter of a century, into the role of a spokesman for radicalism, while Black himself preaches what is for our day orthodox conservative dogma. Douglas speaks of policy goals appropriate to American life in the twenty-first century; Black is avowedly preoccupied with restricting the Court to the support of those human rights that were deemed important in the eighteenth century.

Both the social and the psychological dynamics of the changes that have taken place in the Court, in response to the much more sweeping changes that have been ongoing in the society, are particularly well demonstrated by a set of three correlation matrices which I have prepared, one for the period from 1962 (when White and Goldberg joined the Court) through June 1965; a second, for the next two years, with Fortas replacing Goldberg; and the third matrix for the 1967 and 1968 terms, with Marshall replacing Clark and through Fortas's resignation and Warren's retirement. These matrices measure agreement and disagreement among the justices, across all issues decided on the merits. What the matrices show is that the array of the justices along a general dimension of composite liberalism (both political and economic) was, during the initial period: Douglas, Black, Warren, Brennan, Goldberg, Clark, White, Stewart, and Harlan. Even after a year of Black's deviant behavior, therefore, his consistency during the preceding three years was so great that he still appears in his accustomed position, as the second most liberal member of the Court. This matrix shows two blocs of justices, a liberal bloc ranging from Douglas through Goldberg, and a conservative bloc of the other four. We know, of course, that this finding disguises what was happening during the final year of this period; and there is no doubt that a partitioning of the data into term subsets would reveal that change, and quite sharply.[67] But our second matrix reveals it anyhow: there are, for the 1965 and 1966 terms, still two blocs denoted: Douglas, Fortas, Warren, and Brennan are all positively intercorrelated with each other, and with a single exception negatively otherwise; contrariwise, Clark, White, Stewart, and Harlan are positively intercorrelated with each other, and negatively otherwise. What this implies is that Black was in the middle, negatively correlated with every other member of the Court; and with two minor exceptions—he was .12 with Douglas, and .04 with Stewart—so it was. The reason for his independence we know: his increasing conservatism on many civil liberties and economic questions was countered by his continuing positive support for others, thus bringing him into disagreement, on one issue or another, with everyone else. But by June 1969, Black's transition was complete. The matrix for the last two terms shows a majority bloc, consisting of Fortas, Brennan, Warren, and Marshall; a conservative bloc, consisting of White, Stewart, and Harlan; Douglas, who is isolated in independence on the liberal side of the Fortas bloc; and Black remaining in isolation from both blocs. By the end of the Warren era Black is negatively correlated with everybody except White; Douglas is negatively correlated with everybody except Fortas and Marshall; and it necessarily follows that, for the first time in their twenty-eight years on the Supreme Court together, Douglas and Black were negatively correlated with each other—indeed, Douglas's third largest negative correlation is with Black, and Black's largest negative correlation is with . . . Douglas!

As we have seen, Black's retreat has had little impact upon

the Court's civil liberties policy, because in all except a very few instances there were enough votes, in the new Warren majority, to make decisions without the support of either Black or Douglas. But this makes Black's behavior the more interesting, because his articulation of his new conservative faith has come almost completely in dissenting opinions— it has been, that is to say, largely nonfunctional, so far as concerns the Court's policy output. Why, then, did he do it?

Only by violating Black's own privacy by putting into practice the long-standing advice of Jerome Frank and Harold Lasswell are we likely to be able to answer that sort of question with assurance; but I do have two hypotheses that by no means are necessarily in competition with each other. Both hypotheses postulate obsolescence: the one proffers a sociopsychological explanation of cultural obsolescence, and the other a biological explanation of psychophysiological senescence. I think they reinforce each other, and that in relation to the policy proposal that I am going to advance, it makes no difference which of the two hypothesized variables may be the more important causally, in any particular empirical case (such as Black's).

Black was seventy-eight years old when he began his metamorphosis; the issue that he picked as a turning point clearly has ties that go back to his youthful affiliation with the Ku Klux Klan, and even further to his childhood in a rural Alabama log cabin;[68] and the turning has become progressive, affecting more and more of his work. It is not a crime, or at least not *yet* in the contemporary American polity, for any individual to grow old, even if he is a Supreme Court justice; like birth and death, senescence— whether physiological or psychological—remains for our generation (providing one survives to experience it) a necessity. And it really does not matter, from the point of view of the Supreme Court fulfilling its proper political role as an instrument for the facilitation of controllable change (instead of as the ultimate bastion of social stasis), whether judicial senescence is due primarily to biological aging (as in senility), or (as appears to have been true in the case of Frankfurter) to cultural dissonance reflecting an unbridgeable void between the conceptual world of the elderly judge and that of the political actors who have generated the issues before him for decision. But private vice does *not* produce public virtue; and to perpetuate an institutional arrangement whereby the lives of two hundred million Americans are from time to time made subject to the will of one or more superannuated lawyers *is* a crime—a crime against political society. The humane as well as the sane constitutional policy needed is a rule of compulsory retirement—and for federal judges, presidents, and congressmen alike because the problem is a quite general one.

Black's 1968 TV interview, by Eric Sevareid and Martin Agronsky, is replete with evidence suggestive of Black's aging. Indeed, it is a painful experience to analyze the transcript of the discussion, as I have done. Two well-informed, sensitive, and liberal journalists are engaged in conversation for an hour with a rigid, crotchety, dogmatic old man. Black has always, it is true, been literal minded and unbending[69]—"tough minded," his admirers used to put it—but he did not used to appear confused about simple matters. In the interview, he does such things as to misstate the Court's rule for the order of discussion in conference, and then in the next breath restate what is really the correct rule but in the form of empirical examples, as though he were making a revelation and correcting the misunderstanding of others. Black permitted Agronsky to bait him with a misstatement of the assignment practice (Agronsky asked a question, the premise of which was that the chief justice assigns both majority *and* *minority* opinions), and Black let it stand without correction. But Black's evident confusion about substantive issues, which *are* of some importance, is much more distressing. The man who in his first few months on the Court tried (in a solitary dissent, of course) to get his colleagues to reexamine the question whether business corporations ought to be deemed "persons" within the meaning of the Fourteenth Amendment[70] *now* says that there is no significant difference in the political freedom of citizens to assemble and petition the government, no matter on whose "property" they impose their trespass: Government property does not belong to the citizens who seek to assemble on it to petition for redress of their grievances because—and I quote him exactly, lest I be suspected of exaggeration—"that's not theirs," Black stated; and then repeated, "That's not theirs. It belongs to the government as a whole. Just exactly as a corporation's property belongs to the corporation as a whole." [71]

The whole point of Black's remarks, to the extent that they can be said to have had a consistent theme, was to preserve intact, to enforce to the very letter (the bitter with the better) the political ideas of two centuries ago, and in their most minute details. The Constitution has preserved us; we must preserve it.[72] Surely there is no other way to describe this argument than as a very conservative one. This does not make it wrong, of course, but it does demonstrate how Black's ideology has shifted to remain in touch with the explicit conservative policy goals for which he has voted in recent years. "Change has been said to be truly the law of life but"—he now emphasizes—"sometimes the old and the tried and true are worth holding." [73] There is no important difference between the ideological thrust of either Black's TV testament or his Carpentier Lectures or his recent dissenting opinions, and that of Robert Jackson's posthumously published Godkin Lectures[74]—both Black and Jackson exalt the Constitution, both affirm the separation of powers and reject judicial activism, both argue for a return to law and order (domestic tranquility) and both deemphasize the importance of political freedom as a value that judges can do something positive about.[75] It may not be without significance that when asked in the interview to name the two best lawyers he had known, Black named John W. Davis —a great conservative who argued for the steel companies in the steel seizure decision of 1952, and for the South Carolina and Virginia segregationist respondents in the school segregation decision of 1954—and Bob Jackson, once Black's principal antagonist on the Court, but of whom he now spoke with affection. And when asked to name a non-lawyer who might have made a good Supreme Court justice, Black's ideal was Walter Lippmann.

It is a supreme irony that Hugo Black's problem is that he has become too old for the job. That was precisely Franklin Roosevelt's complaint against the Hughes Court, and it was to break the grip of gerontocracy upon the Supreme Court that Black was appointed to it. But Black and Frankfurter, the two men whom Roosevelt thought best symbolized the liberalism of the New Deal, both ended up as great dissenters[76]—great *conservative* dissenters—and both literally and figuratively, as Old Dealers. Franklin Roosevelt, however unwittingly, was probably correct in attacking the Hughes Court for its age, instead of for its conservatism.

CHAPTER III

THE

AMERICAN POLITY

We live in an age of revolution. Except for the very eldest among us, we cannot even remember a time when war was not either an omnipresent threat, or else a preemptive reality —save during our childhood, when some of us dwelt in a world that is now gone forevermore, a time when not just the urban ghettos and rural slums housed the relatively poor, but rather a time when almost everyone was absolutely poor for a while. And many then were cold, and many were hungry—not just hungry for TV with color, nor for four on the floor, nor even for psychic nourishment but rather for food—just as most of the people in the world today remain poor, illhoused, and worse fed. Most Americans today are better off economically than was the generation that brought Franklin Roosevelt into the White House, with the promise of a New Deal for all. But the New Deal was over even before the Nazis invaded Austria, slipping rapidly into our cultural memory as one of that trilogy of fleeting periods—the others being Wilson's New Freedom, and Jack Kennedy's New Frontier—when ideals (and, to a limited extent, action) of political, social, and economic liberalism were a major concern of domestic politics for the nation's leadership. Sandwiched between World War II and the Korean War was a brief encounter with an administration that called itself—and under the circumstances then prevailing in Washington, somewhat incongruously—the Fair Deal; and since Dallas, we have come to experience the kind of national domestic leadership that can be, and no doubt for the foreseeable short-range future can continue to be, characterized as simply "the Deal."

One by one, we have seen the demographic models of the American populace atrophy and disappear from the face of the land, as viable social and economic empirical units: first the family farm, then the city, now the metropolis. The young people who today seek so desperately to distinguish themselves from the custodians of a society that they regard (and perhaps with considerable justification) as sick—sick politically, socially, economically, and psychologically—are the heirs to Hiroshima and Nagasaki; and from the time when they first experienced even minimal political awareness, there has not been a moment when the possibility of having their world blow up could be discounted as romantic, or even as highly improbable. "Fail-Safe" and "Dr. Strangelove" symbolize a way of life that has virtually no communality with that of "The Bobbsey Twins at the Seashore." Even the proudest products of our economic affluence, ranging from our houses to our clothes and our automobiles, are built to break down, so that the maintenance and replacement markets can continue to expand. And we must not forget the education of our young: first the grade schools, then the high schools, next the colleges, and now even the graduate departments of what once were thought to be great universities, each in its turn has become an elaborate and extraordinarily expensive custodial institution, providing baby-sitting services for the children of working parents, almost from the cradle to what is often today long past the altar. (This is a service well known to our society, but it used to be provided only by private schools, and for the offspring of the well-to-do.) I select only a few of the more conspicuous from among an almost unlimited array of possible examples of decadence, deliberate destruction, and demoralization—and I do not for an instant mean to imply that our problems are parochial, or that they can be attributed to causes peculiar to American culture.

Such is the background for militant advocacy of revolutionary change. Black power, student power, peace power, these are the watchwords of the multifarious radical factions who insist that political freedom, social freedom, economic freedom, and psychological freedom *now* are the indispensable conditions for the establishment of justice, the promotion of the general welfare, and the securing of the blessings of liberty;[1] and that to whatever extent may be necessary such other constitutional goals as the assurance of domestic tranquility and provision for the common defense must be foregone, or even repudiated, in order to maximize the scope and the extent of radical redistribution of our assets as a nation, in relation to the three criteria of Justice, Welfare, and Liberty. There is nothing novel, of course, about the manipulation of such ideological symbols as these, for purposes either of fomenting or of rationalizing the outcomes of a revolution. Liberty and Welfare and Justice, as well as Tranquility and Defense—all of these combine, and with equal authority in their documentary context, to define the goals of the nation in the Preamble to the Constitution for the United States of America. There is one other clause of the Preamble, "to form a more perfect Union," which I have not mentioned heretofore because it does not seem yet to have become as seriously at issue, in contemporary American politics, as have the other five; that situation is of course very different in countries with a less homogeneous political culture, such as Canada where cultural dichotomization does largely coincide with geographic boundaries.

In a very fundamental sense, to speak of the revolutionary components of American society today, including the relation between radical ideologies and constitutional ideals, is to define the "living Constitution," [2] for in this broader sense the Constitution of the United States is not the document, but rather it is the way in which Americans live in relation to each other.[3] And as Chief Justice Earl Warren has assured us, early in his tenure on the Court but after he had made the pregnant decision to move to the left closer to Black and Douglas, Supreme Court justices themselves are "not monks or scientists, but participants in the living stream of our national life." [4]

There are three questions that I shall endeavor to explore concerning the participatory role of the justices in the mainstream of American political life. The first question relates to why the Court has changed, in the way and to the extent that I have described in the two previous chapters. The second question directs our inquiry into the constraints imposed upon the Court by such other components of the regime as public opinion, political parties and interest groups, the legal profession and lower courts, Congress and the administration, and state governments. The third question asks what have been the consequences, for significant social groupings in American society, of the Supreme Court's professed policies during the present century—to what extent, why, and with what results have those persons supposedly affected by the Court's decisions complied with the norms of behavior that the Court has posited for them? To put the matter in a way that some may consider to be more jargonistic, we shall seek to examine the principal interaction effects between Supreme Court justices and other major actors in the American polity.

Why Has the Supreme Court Changed Its Policies?

Of course, the easiest answer to this question is that the Court has changed its policies because the justices themselves have changed; and the liberal thrust of the Court's policies during the past three decades is due to the appointment of more liberal justices. In effect, this is the answer that I gave in the second chapter. Such an explanation is true, but not completely satisfying, for we are left with the next obvious question: then why these more liberal justices? Why not more Van Devanters and McReynolds and Sutherlands? Certainly, the last-named trio is considerably more representative, as a sample of the universe of ninety-six individuals who (by June 1969) had acted as Supreme Court justices, than would be Brandeis and Holmes and Stone, to take the other wing of the Taft Court.

The manifest reason why we have not had more Van Devanters and Sutherlands is that from Coolidge until Nixon we had no conservative Republican presidents, such as Taft and Harding, to appoint right-wing Republican justices. President Harding supplied three of the Four Horsemen of the Hughes Court, plus Taft himself as the chief during the twenties, for good measure. But there have been only four Republican presidents since Harding; and Coolidge's only chance was wasted, from our present perspective, upon Stone. The next two Republicans, Hoover and Eisenhower, were both moderates within the political spectra of their party—let us not forget that Eisenhower's main competitor for the party nomination was William Howard Taft's son—and their own choices tended to cancel out, ranging from liberal (Cardozo, Warren, Brennan) through moderate (Hughes, Stewart) to conservative (Harlan, Whittaker). The overall impact of the selections of Coolidge, Hoover, and Eisenhower clearly has been much more liberal than conservative, both quantitatively and qualitatively. Nixon, however, is committed to pack the Court with reactionaries so as to redress the libertarian excesses of the Warren Court; and his nominations of Warren Earl Burger and G. Harrold Carswell, to replace Earl Warren and Abe Fortas, can only be viewed as faithful fulfillment of his campaign promises.

The only other consistently conservative choices have been those of Harry Truman; and these can be charged up as part of the civilian sacrifices required to support the war effort—because Roosevelt's decision to dump Henry Wallace in favor of Truman certainly represented an effort to maintain a united war front, by building bridges with both the South and Congress, at whatever sacrifice might be necessary of domestic, civilian, and peacetime values. Indeed, I would argue that the latent cause of conservative Supreme Court appointments, during the past half century, has been war. Harding (with his cohort Coolidge) was elected in a reaction against American involvement in World War I; Truman because of World War II; Eisenhower because of the Korean War; and Nixon because of the Vietnam War. Hoover, Roosevelt, Kennedy, and Johnson assumed the presidency on the basis of what were primarily domestic concerns, and the balance of their appointments clearly was on the liberal side. Note that the really conservative appointments—those by Harding, by Truman, and by Nixon —came, in each instance, on the heels of, and in the period of reaction against, American involvement in a major war. (It is intriguing, in this regard, to contemplate the retrojection of this hypothesis to include the Chase Court and the postbellum period of Reconstruction; and its projection to the additional appointments that will probably be forthcoming from President Nixon.)

Only part of the cost of war is paid in conservative staffing of the Court, however. In addition, there is the pervasive influence that any period of war has in disrupting the economy, uprooting large segments of the society, and most important of all, in substituting in place of civil liberties authoritarian controls over the behavior of the military and civilians alike. The effect of this kind of political milieu is to generate issues stemming from the deprivations of freedom that are the felt necessities of wartime; and invariably, the Supreme Court's response is to decide much more conservatively a smaller number of civil liberties claims; and even these claims concern attempts to resist encroachments upon what previously had been recognized as personal rights and liberties. Wars do not lead to Supreme Court decisions that extend the limits of human freedom. The Vietnam War may seem to be an exception, because of the high tide of libertarianism on the Court during the period of the past half dozen years; but the obvious explanation is that its effect upon civilians has been indirect thus far. Moreover, the effects of the war have been antilibertarian, by diverting a major portion of the national budget away from needed social and economic reconstruction, by fomenting massive anxiety and insecurity among the nation's youth, and as a direct by-product of these first two causes, by fostering the growth of radical ideologies and sociopolitical movements that constitute a much greater threat to civil liberties in the United States than conservatism ever has posed within our lifetime. By radical I mean explicitly to refer both to the radical left, as exemplified by Maoists and Guaverists, as well as to the radical right, such as Minutemen and American Nazis. Thus violence feeds upon itself; and one of the problems with which we increasingly are going to be confronted, and one that the Supreme Court can neither prevent nor solve for us is that, in the words of Robert Jackson, "No mob has ever protected any liberty, even its own. . . . The crowd mind . . . does not want a tolerant effort at meeting of minds. It does not know the futility of trying to mob an idea. Released from the sense of personal responsibility that would restrain even the worst individuals in it if alone and brave with the courage of numbers, both radical and reactionary mobs endanger liberty as well as order." [5]

But war is not the only irrational cause of change in the Court. Chance, too, plays a continuing part in human affairs, and often constitutes a much larger influence than is recognized or acknowledged.[6] John Clarke's premature and voluntary retirement, no matter how rational it seemed to him in psychological terms, was certainly an unpredictable and unexpected, and therefore a chance event, from a social point of view. Or take the sudden deaths of Murphy and Rutledge, the two most committed civil libertarians ever to sit upon the Court, both still relatively young—only in their fifties—and both during the same summer vacation. Their conjoint passing was a lucky break for McCarthyism, but a most unfortunate one for American civil liberties.

On the other hand, Taft's continuing efforts to exert maximal influence upon the staffing of the Supreme Court, over a period of more than two decades in his various roles as president, law-professor-in-waiting, and chief justice, stand out as the most consistently rational factor affecting change in the Supreme Court that there probably has ever been. Moreover, Chief Justice Taft did not confine his lobbying efforts to the personnel aspects of controlling change in the Court. He attempted also to affect the posture in which issues would be presented to the Court, and the way in which the Court's policies would be received, by influencing the staffing of the lower federal courts, and by welding the entire federal judiciary into one cohesive team, over which he, as chief justice, would of course preside. His initial plans, in 1921–1922, included a provision for extending the principle of executive leadership of the judiciary by the use of itinerant federal judges, to be dispatched by the chief to roam among the circuits, dispensing the Court's justice where it was most needed. This part of the plan did not win acceptance at the time, but other aspects did, such as the national conference of federal judges, under the direction of the chief, to develop uniform rules of internal policy for the federal courts. Even more important was the Judges' Bill which Taft had drafted by the Court and which he then guided through the legislative process in Congress.[7] Enacted in 1925, this statute delegated to the Court almost complete discretion to decide which cases—and therefore, which issues—it would select to consider on the merits, and when it would choose to do so. It is hard to overemphasize the importance of this development as a giant step in the direction of enhancing the Court's policy-making opportunities and capabilities. Fifty years earlier in 1875, for example, two-thirds of the cases decided by the Supreme Court were concerned with either "common" (i.e., state) law issues, or with such federal specialties as admiralty, bankruptcy, patents, claims against the federal government, and conflicts over title to public lands claims. Only a tenth related to constitutionality, taxation, or other "public law" questions.[8] (This, incidentally, is still the kind of policy configuration that one encounters even today in the highest courts of other federal common-law countries, such as the Supreme Court of Canada or the High Court of Australia, which lack the authority to manipulate the policy content of their own dockets.) By 1925, the year in which Taft's bill was enacted, the same major grouping of common law plus the federal specialties and federal claims had shrunk from two-thirds but was still over 40 per cent; governmental regulation of the economy and taxation constituted another 40 per cent; and claims to personal rights of all types (including those of criminal defendants in prohibition cases) accounted for less than a fifth of the Taft Court's work. The proportions today are about three-fourths personal rights, a fifth economic regulation and taxation, and the remaining 5 per cent or less is all the attention that is given to the federal claims and specialties. Common-law issues virtually have disappeared except for an occasional diversity jurisdiction case taken to resolve intercircuit conflict. But the point is that one important reason why the Warren Court could spend three-fourths of its time on civil liberties policy is because Taft worked so hard to restructure the institutional norms so as to make possible such a result, even though under Warren it was hardly in the direction Taft intended.

Even in the physical symbolization of the Court's role and work, Taft did much to create conditions that would help to enhance the effectiveness of policy developments along directions that he, Taft, feared and hated. Both of his two immediate predecessors, Fuller and White, had turned down the new Supreme Court building that President Taft had offered them gratis: he would have been happy to make all arrangements, if only a chief justice could have been found to accept his munificence, but they stubbornly preferred the squatters' rights in the Capitol to an independent edifice that would have proclaimed their autonomy as the third branch of the government. But in the very years that his Judges' Bill was adopted, opportunity knocked for Taft to step up his campaign for the new building; now as chief justice he persuaded Congress to give him the marble palace that less far-sighted men had spurned a generation earlier.[9] Of course, he did not expect to, and did not in fact, live to see the result. But in 1935, less than a year and a half before F.D.R.'s attack, the Hughes Court did move into the new building, which Taft's prescience had made available at just the right time to serve as a forum in which the Roosevelt Court could begin to remake the nation's constitutional policies.

How Is the Court Constrained by the Political Regime?

I am not going to dwell upon the theme that the Supreme Court has neither the purse nor the sword, because it seems to me that our recent history is replete with evidence that in regard to the use of what surely is the biggest purse known to mankind—even if there may be some doubt concerning whether the sword is only number two, and perhaps not even trying harder at that—the persons who have the biggest say do not necessarily get their way in the world, or even in this country, for that matter. So I am going to entertain the alternative hypothesis, that the restraints imposed upon Supreme Court justices, by the political regime, differ more in degree than in kind from those that apply also to such other political actors as congressmen and the president.

The most general and diffuse form of restraint, but perhaps the most fundamental of all, is that to which we refer as public opinion: mass attitudes toward the decisional role of the Court. Only very recently has any attention been paid to this question,[10] but the half dozen reports that have appeared, all within the past three years, do pretty much agree upon certain basic findings.

In two recent national cross-sectional surveys of the adult population of the United States, taken immediately after the 1964 and 1966 elections by the University of Michigan's

Survey Research Center, less than half of the respondents could identify any particular decision or policy of the Supreme Court that they either liked or disliked.[11] (Moreover, a substantial minority—about a third—of those who did profess to explicit views were mistaken about the position that they attributed to the Court, blaming it for having "gotten mixed up in this war" or praising it because "they gave us medicare" or otherwise on irrelevant grounds.) An even smaller minority of the total sample, about 40 per cent, could suggest (in their own words, to an open-end question) anything that, by latitudinarian construction, could be interpreted to signify at least minimal awareness of the Court's policy-making role. Those who were both aware of the Court's role and knowledgeable about some specific example of it constituted only a fourth (27 per cent) of the total sample. Of various relations between what was claimed to be specific knowledge about the Court, and other background variables concerning the respondents, the only correlations that were even moderately high were with education and with an index of "alienation from government," variables which were also moderately and positively correlated with each other. All three of these intercorrelations were around .40; the highest correlation in the matrix was .69, between alienation and knowledge of party control in the House of Representatives. So the relatively well-educated persons who had the most specific knowledge about the Court also were high in their more general (if elementary) political knowledge, but they were negative in their orientation toward the government (that is, in 1966, toward the Johnson administration).

This study by Walter Murphy and Joseph Tanenhaus examines also both diffuse and specific attitudes of support towards the Court. The relevant minority was about the same size as that aware of the Court's role, with 37 per cent of the sample indicating a generally favorable disposition toward the Court—and these constitute a majority of those who take a position either pro or con, because 40 per cent of the sample were either undecided or unclassifiable. However, the proportion of the total sample who have both general and specific knowledge about the Court, and who also give it diffuse support, drops to 13 per cent. Clearly, as the authors of the study point out, most of the persons who support the Court in a general way do so primarily, if not strictly, from ignorance. But lowest of all was specific support for the Court's policies: disregarding the accuracy of the respondents' information, and scoring simply on the basis of how many explicit things they said they liked or disliked about what the Court had done recently, the ratio of negative to positive specifics was over three to one, with less than 10 per cent of the total sample naming explicit (whether real or imagined) Court acts which were deemed to be favorable. As one might expect, almost all of this relatively highly engaged minority, 7 per cent of the total sample, are also positive on diffuse support; and indeed there are another 10 per cent who are positive in their diffuse support *even though* they are negative in specific support, which means, quite simply, that the justices are receiving more general allegiance from persons who *dis*agree than they get from persons who agree with them! On the other hand, virtually none (much less than 1 per cent) take the position which would have to be either quite irrational or else quite sophisticated, of liking the particulars of the Court's work while disapproving of it in general. The observation of this zero cell establishes, and with statistical significance (given the sample size of over a thousand), that the relation between diffuse and specific support for the Court is a scale in the Guttman or cumulative sense: that is, all persons who support, on balance, the Court's particular policies will also support the Court as an institution; but the converse does not necessarily hold because of that even larger number who disagree on the outputs but still support the institution. Murphy and Tanenhaus do not report the proportion of persons who are aware of both the Court's policies and its role, and who support it both in those policies and in its role; but it is quite apparent from their data that this cannot be more than 2 to 3 per cent of the total sample. Readers of this book, that is to say, are extremely atypical of most of their fellow citizens, in their knowledge about and in their attitude toward the Court.

The only explicit demographic distinction that the authors discuss or report (and then only fragmentarily) is to confirm that, however ironic it might seem, most Negroes, whom the authors identify as "the group of people who have benefited most obviously from the Court's activity in recent years," are completely unaware of the Court, although for the "very few" (and I quote the authors' words, because they report no numbers on this) who are knowledgeable, 90 per cent give the Court diffuse support (and probably, although the report does not say so, specific support as well).[12]

Kenneth Dolbeare has examined similar data, but from the point of view of the relative attitudes of trust and support by the public toward the Supreme Court in relation to the president and the Congress. He finds first of all, when asked which branch of the national government "does the most important things," that a majority of a statewide sample of Wisconsin adults (in 1966) thought that Congress did, with a quarter preferring the president, and only 6 per cent choosing the Supreme Court, which ran a poor third. Similarly, the Wisconsin sample had by far *the least confidence* in the Supreme Court, as compared to Congress and the president; and only in regard to the Court was there a negative balance of confidence. (And this survey was made,

I repeat, in 1966, when Lyndon Johnson's presidency was well into its denouement, the Congress was Democratic, and the Court itself was Democratic by a two-to-one ratio.) When the respondents were classified according to party, Democrats and Independents and Republicans alike had confidence in Congress; Democrats had, but Republicans lacked, confidence in the president; while Independents had more confidence in the Court than either Democrats or Republicans, but even among the Independents, there were more who lacked confidence in the Court than who had it. These findings led Dolbeare to conclude that the Court is widely perceived to be "relatively unimportant and relatively untrustworthy." [13] Dolbeare confirms the substantial ignorance about the Court, showing that in response to an array of eight issues—half of them phony—concerning which the Court purportedly had been making policy, an average of almost half the sample (over 40 per cent) could not answer about any of these matters, and only two were clearly distinguished correctly: school prayer and school segregation (by identical divisions of over 70 per cent who said that the Court had made decisions on these subjects, to only 7 per cent who thought otherwise). The next two most popular issues were spurious (medicare, and federal aid to education); and even though we may explain the circumstance, that claims to knowledge were almost as high for what the Court did not do as for what it did, as a consequence of the "halo effect" created by the many persons who were unwilling to admit, or unable to distinguish, their own ignorance, the fact remains that an average of only between 10 to 15 per cent of the total sample did differentiate between fact and fiction in the Court's work.[14] But knowledge was negatively correlated with approval of the Court: those with the best knowledge were least approving, especially among Republicans, and those most ignorant about its work were most favorably disposed toward the Court.[15] In short, debate and discussion about the Court is a proclivity for the intelligentsia, and is simply lost upon most Americans, who support the Court as a cultural symbol like the flag or the national anthem—and understand it no better.

A subsequent study by Dolbeare, in collaboration with sociologist Phillip Hammond, suggests that there may yet be one strand of rationality—party identification—linking the Court to its mass audience. An examination of the results of eight surveys over a period of a quarter of a century (1941–1966) leads these authors to conclude that "Democrats are distinctly more favorable toward the Court than are Republicans, except when there is a Republican President" and that "for the great majority of people, party—as party, not as a surrogate for ideology or socio-economic status—is, together with Presidential incumbency, the dominant source of cues for attitudes toward the Court." [16] The correlation between high knowledge and status, and low esteem for the Court, is shown (these authors claim) to be spurious, when party identification is controlled statistically, because of the well understood tendency for the Democratic party to appeal more strongly than the Republican to the relatively more numerous persons in the lowest social, economic, and educational strata. But I think it is fair to conclude, on the basis of what has been published thus far, that more (and more sophisticated) work utilizing statistical methods of causal and path analysis is needed before we can have very much confidence either in the proposition that the justices ride the president's coattails for their mass support, or in the alternative hypothesis that to know the Court is to loathe it.

When we turn from party followership to party leadership, then it is of course quite clear that the Supreme Court always has been in politics, in the most basic sense that the Court has been recurringly a controversial issue between the two major parties of the day, since its establishment in 1790. At the very time when Taft was integrating his team on the Court, Senator LaFollette and other progressives of the early twenties were launching in national periodicals, speeches, the Progressive party platform, and on the floor of Congress, an attack upon the Supreme Court's usurpations of legislative authority. Taft called radicals such as George Norris "blatherskites," and by 1928 had begun to refer to the United States Senate as "a Bolshevik body." [17] Not long thereafter, the opposition to the Hughes and Parker nominations was (like Taft's own remarks) ideological rather than partisan, although Franklin Roosevelt's attack in 1937 certainly was both. On the other hand, the congressional agitation of 1957–1959 can hardly be seen as partisan, because it was led by Republicans, at a time when a Republican was president, against a Court led by a Republican chief and composed of as many Republicans as Democrats.[18] In the 1959 vote on House Resolution No. 3, then the key legislative proposal to restrain the Court, the percentage of Republicans voting in favor of the measure (79 per cent) was twice as large as the percentage of Democrats so doing (41 per cent). Evidently, these same data support an ideological interpretation of the division, because these ratios correspond to the proportions, at that time, of conservatives within the Republican party and of their counterparts (almost exclusively Southerners) within the Democratic party. But in the 1964 presidential campaign, it is quite clear that the Republican candidate did make what, in the light of his own political role at the time, must be construed (like Roosevelt's in 1937) as in part a partisan attack, although the focus of his bill of particulars was strictly ideological. Goldwater explicitly criticized the Court's

policies on school prayers, reapportionment, and fair procedure for criminal defendants; but he took no stand on
racial equality or other civil libertarian issues. Johnson refused to debate the issue, and only a few Democratic politi-
cians—persons who, like the late Robert Kennedy and
Robert Wagner, were not closely identified with the administration—did speak out in defense of the Court. A recent
study of Goldwater's efforts, to pick up (or to catalyze)
conservative support by attacking the Court's liberalism,
reports on the basis of national survey data a very modest
positive correlation of .33 between supporting Goldwater
and disapproving (in discrete comments) the Court.[19] The
authors discount the likelihood that Goldwater's efforts
could have had much influence upon public attitudes toward reapportionment or fair procedure, because of the slight
public awareness of either issue; and they have no evidence
to demonstrate whatever effect (if any) Goldwater may have
had in stimulating opposition to the Court on religious
freedom. They do suggest, however, that the fact that a
"late September poll, taken after Goldwater began his Court
criticism, showed a substantial increase over August in concern expressed over race relations," [20] is evidence that
Goldwater had some success in arousing opposition to the
Court on the issue of racial equality. I find this inference
unpersuasive in view of the statement, earlier in the same
article, that "the Senator took great pains to avoid any explicit attack on decisions affecting the rights of Negroes." [21]
I am also unconvinced, on the basis of the evidence reported
or discussed, that this study shows that "the Senator did
articulate, mobilize, and legitimize conservative sentiment
against the Court." [22] Goldwater certainly articulated, tried
to mobilize, and tried to legitimize conservative sentiment.
Part, but by no means all or even most, of that conservative
sentiment was against the Court, but for reasons that owe

nothing directly to Goldwater. The extent to which he had any effects whatsoever upon public attitudes toward the Supreme Court remains, I submit, a wide open question. The authors do point out, and rightly so, that Goldwater may well have alienated more support than he attracted for his own cause, by his attacks on the Court. If his impact upon public attitudes toward the Court was no greater than his impact upon public voting at the polls, it could not have been very much.

The Court has also long been involved in interest-group politics, with both friends and foes of greater or lesser constancy, quite apart from those which have been its conspicuous litigational clients.[23] Taft considered farmers, laborers, widows, and veterans all to be "anti-Court" in their orientation.[24] On the other hand, business and manufacturing groups such as the NAM, the Chamber of Commerce of the United States, and the American Liberty League rallied strongly to the defense of the Hughes Court in 1937; so, in this instance, did the National Grange, and America Forward (an ephemeral religious acolyte of the Republican party); while merely lip service was given to F.D.R.'s Court plan by the CIO and AFL, with the Farm Bureau Federation remaining ostentatiously neutral; and only such groups as the Communist party, Labor's Nonpartisan League, and the liberal intellectual weeklies *Nation* and *The New Republic*, really tried to support F.D.R. on this issue.[25] According to Walter Murphy, the most influential groups in the 1957–1959 campaign against the Court were the FBI, the NAM, and the AFL-CIO, and in that order.[26] Only the FBI succeeded in getting legislation through Congress at this time; the FBI bill was to modify by limiting the so-called Jencks Rule of the Court, the effect of which was to open to cross-examination the previously confidential basis underlying the written reports on investigations made by the bureau's agents. Business and labor had, of course, changed sides since 1937; now it was the AFL-CIO that defended, while the NAM attacked, the Court. Less effective were the NAACP, American Civil Liberties Union, Americans for Democratic Action, and the American Veterans Committee, all pro-Court; and the Chamber of Commerce of the United States, the American Farm Bureau Federation, and the International Association of Police Chiefs, all anti-Court. Still other groups, such as the American Bar Association and the Catholic church, found it impossible to take a clear-cut position regarding the reform of the Court at this time, because of the sharp division within their respective leadership hierarchies. But in addition to those groups which exercised some direct influence upon the decisions being made in Congress concerning the Court, or at least attempted to do so, there were many other groups that directed their efforts at attempts to influence public opinion rather than the votes of congressmen directly. Most of these publicity-oriented groups were right-wing critics of the Court, and they included various White Citizens Councils, the John Birch Society, the Christian Crusade (to impeach Earl Warren), the Manion Forum, SPX Research Associates—that SPX stands for "Soviet Principle 10" and one of their publications is a study entitled "The Supreme Court as an Instrument of Global Conquest" (that really boggles the mind, doesn't it? Today, the world; tomorrow?)—Dan Smoot, the National Economic Council, the American Coalition of Patriotic Societies, the DAR, the VFW, the American Legion, *U.S. News and World Report*, William Buckley and his *National Review, Farm and Ranch Magazine,* and so on and on.[27] In view of the evidence, from Murphy's case study, that congressmen paid virtually no attention to the radical right, and the evidence from survey research studies indicating that anti-Court opinions are held by a relatively well-informed and well-educated audience—manifestly, a very different kind of audience than that to which most of the radical right directs its message—the necessary conclusion is that the pay-off for all of this frenetic activity, measured in terms of influence upon the Court, must have been very small indeed.

The organized legal profession can be viewed as a set of groups that usually maintain a special interest in the activities of courts, including the Supreme Court. The bar associations can also be seen as instruments through which other groups and individuals, such as business and political leaders, work to attempt to maintain indirectly an influence over the judiciary. For example, not only business groups were disenchanted with the Supreme Court after 1937. Lloyd Wells has pointed out that "the gigantic public relations campaign 'to sell free enterprise to the American people' dates from this period," and "as the judges moved away from constitutional doctrines which had served business interests so well in the past, they lost powerful and articulate support within the business community, the legal profession, and the press, the very groups traditionally responsible for perpetuating the orthodox juristic tradition." [28] Hardly a year had elapsed after the Roberts switch before the then ABA president was publicly deploring the Court's abdication of its responsibilities, and the *American Bar Association Journal* was publishing editorials exhorting the bar to mobilize in defense of the Bill of Rights—and the explicit reference was to the *Tenth* Amendment. Nor did the ABA limit itself to ideological disputation; also in 1939, its House of Delegates approved a recommendation from the Committee on Judicial Salaries, previously bullish on that subject, that further increases for federal judges be deferred until the federal budget could be balanced.[29] But much more fundamental, imaginative, and enduring action was taken after the end of World War II, when some old Republican pros decided to penetrate the ABA and use it as a front to compensate for their own relative ineffectiveness—given the Senate's own policy of permitting state delegations to exercise the predominant voice in regard to nominations to the lower courts—during the fourth successive term under a Democratic president. The then chairman of the Senate Judiciary Committee was Alexander Wiley, a Republican from Wisconsin and a former president of the ABA, who lamented in the *ABA Journal* that "the present political character of the members [of] the federal bench is grossly lopsided on the side of Democratic Leftists." As a remedy, he proposed that the ABA itself set up a committee to screen the legal qualifications of presidential nominations to the courts, promising that his own committee of the Senate would cooperate fully in such a step.[30] The ABA did set up the committee; and although there were some ups and downs in the early years, especially when the Democrats regained control over the Senate, the Eisenhower administration granted the committee access to the nomination process in the Department of Justice, which put the ABA in the much stronger position of being able to exercise influence over the choice among candidates, instead of just attempting to veto presidential choices already decided upon; and under Eisenhower even Supreme Court nominations were referred to the ABA committee for advice.[31]

During the 1957–1959 attacks on the Warren Court, the ABA was divided between a minority—mostly law professors—who wanted the organization to support the Court, and a majority who preferred to condemn it. In 1956 the House of Delegates refused to approve a supportive manifesto sponsored by a group of one hundred lawyers who sought to defend the Court against "reckless" attacks.[32] But in the following year the House of Delegates refused also to recommend that Congress enact legislation to reverse the Court, and in 1958 the House of Delegates voted to oppose the approval by Congress of the leading anti-Court bill then under consideration. In 1959, however, approval was given to a set of resolutions,[33] emanating from the Committee on Communist Tactics, Strategy and Objectives, that put the ABA on record as supporting congressional enactment of legislation to overcome the Warren Court's decisions that had encouraged the Communist conspiracy in its subversive efforts.[34] The effect that delegate approval of these resolutions might have had was to some degree mitigated by the circumstance that the incumbent ABA president in 1958 was Charles Rhyne, a liberal who did his best to create the impression that the ABA was not really as critical of the Court as might seem to some to be the case.[35]

The response of lower court judges to Supreme Court policy making has varied with the issue. Lower court cooperation probably was greatest in regard to reapportionment, an issue which thrust both state and federal judges throughout the country into the heady role of kingmakers in drawing the lines for local political controversy for the next decade or so, a temptation which very few judges gave any public indication of fighting very hard to resist. Racial equality, and particularly in relation to the desegregation of public schools in the South, was quite another matter. Peltason has described the varying degrees of opposition, to the Supreme Court's own policy, that came from the federal district judges whose own residence, ties, and sympathies tended to be most closely (at least, in comparison with other federal judges) identified with the prosegregation communities in which social and political resistance was greatest on this issue. Let us take Dallas as an example. The brunt of opposition to the Supreme Court was shouldered, during the fifties, by two rabidly segregationist federal judges: an eighty-eight-year-old Harding Republican, William Atwell, whose successor in the same role was his staunch political foe, T. Whitfield Davidson, an eighty-two-year-old Democrat; six times in as many years the federal courts of appeals reversed decisions by these octogenarian impedimenta, and seven years after *Brown* v. *Board of Education* the federal district court in Dallas remained completely successful in preventing even a beginning toward school desegregation there.[36] But Kenneth Vines has shown that during the first eight and one-half years after the Court's 1954 decision, not only did a majority of the race relations cases, in the southern federal district courts, relate to education (as distinguished from access to government facilities, voting, transportation, trial procedures, employment, and other claims); also a higher proportion of cases (61 per cent) were decided favorably to racial equality in the education cases than in any of the other categories.[37] Moreover, Vines reported that the demographic basis for judicial behavior seemed to be no different from that for other forms of political behavior: the correlation between Negro population density and judicial outcomes favorable to racial equality was —.48, while the correlation between Negro population density and Negro registration was —.46.[38] Vines has also shown that the federal courts of appeals, during this same period, and necessarily in relation to the same universe of cases, upheld claims to racial equality at a rate half again greater than that for the district courts (75 per cent as compared to 51 per cent); and that in the southern state supreme courts, the rate dropped to 29 per cent.[39] Further analysis of these state decisions showed that the rate was almost twice as high (about 40 per cent) for desegregation actions as it was for appeals from convictions for sit-ins and demonstrations and for state action against organizations supporting racial equality.

Appeals on racial discrimination grounds by criminal defendants were of course over ten times as frequent in state supreme as in federal district courts; disregarding them, the proportions of Negro to white initiators of actions in the remaining more general civil rights cases were: 27 per cent black, 40 per cent white (state); and 87 per cent black, 10 per cent white (federal). No matter what allowance one makes for jurisdictional and other legal differences, this greater than three-to-one preference of Negro claimants for federal courts and the four-to-one preference of white litigants for state courts suggest that all expected Negroes to receive fairer treatment in federal than in state courts. Vines concludes, however, that with the fair procedure cases eliminated from the samples, the difference between the degrees of support given to racial equality by state and by federal judges in the South is in fact relatively small—evidently, within the range of 10 to 15 per cent higher for the federal district judges; and that in some states, Negroes "fared better in state court than in the federal courts." According to Mitau, there was strong consensus among the southern judiciary, with three-fourths of the decisions of the local courts affirmed upon appeal to the state supreme courts. However, Vines indicates that in the racial equality cases in which state supreme courts did reverse lower courts, 94 per cent were in favor of the civil rights claimants—a percentage identical to that reported by Mitau as the rate of reversal, between 1960 and 1966, by the United States Supreme Court of state supreme court decisions unfavorable to Negro defendants in cases involving trespass and breach of peace convictions of civil rights demonstrators. Upon remand in one group of the latter cases, the state supreme courts reaffirmed 80 per cent of their own prior decisions, only to be reversed again in subsequent appeals.[40] On the whole, it does seem clear that the southern state supreme courts were less supportive of racial equality than the federal district courts in the same region; and that the local state courts in the South were least in agreement, and in compliance, with the United States Supreme Court.

Further evidence of the alienation of state judiciaries, from the United States Supreme Court, is provided by the manifesto, agreed to by an overwhelming majority of 36–8 of the Conference of Chief Justices of State Supreme Courts, in the midst of the attack on the Warren Court.[41] These resolutions are couched in the rhetoric of states' rights, but the empirical evidence which they cite and discuss focuses upon the same Warren Court decisions, relating to political freedom and fair procedure, that were then under attack in the Congress; and although there is no explicit reference to racial equality, it seems likely "that much of the conference's criticism could be attributed to lingering dissatisfaction with the School Segregation cases. Undoubtedly the Southern bloc constituted a formidable pressure group within the state judges' conference." [42] But the timing was bad; the decision of the state chief justices came on August 23, 1958, the last full day of the session for the Eighty-fifth Congress,[43] thereby forestalling until the following year whatever political effect it might have upon the outcome of the anti-Court bills.

Although a certain amount of congressional reversal of the Court is not unusual,[44] that is to be distinguished from the events of 1957–1959, when the focus of reform was upon the Court's political leadership rather than being directed against a more discrete aspect of substantive (and particularly, of statutory) policy. Actually, the only relevant legislation then adopted, the FBI sponsored anti-Jencks bill, was ambiguous in terms of this distinction: it was more of a codification of the Court's decision, limiting possibly euphoric future interpretation, than a reversal;[45] and it was not ostensibly a rebuke to the Court. But the bills that did not pass were straightforward enough, and so was the debate concerning them. They dealt with six principal issues, all of which were reactions against explicit recent decisions of the Warren Court relating to either political freedom or to fair procedure: admission to law practice, legislative investigations, executive loyalty programs, state control of subversion, teacher loyalty, and the denial of passports on loyalty grounds. A coalition of conservative Republicans and Southern Democrats pushed several bills through the House of Representatives during the summer of 1958, but Lyndon Johnson, in his role of majority leader, became the instrument for forging the recommitment of the two leading bills, by a one vote margin; and then the threat of a Wayne Morse filibuster catalyzed an agreement to defeat the remaining (the anti-*Mallory*) bill, on a procedural technicality for which the formal decision was pronounced as a ruling on a point of order by the then vice-president, Richard Nixon. The Court's retreat in June 1959, consequent to Frankfurter's switch, precluded the possibility of getting the Senate to reconsider its decision of the previous year; the same array of bills passed the House again, but never got out of committee in the Senate.[46]

Except for the federal Omnibus Crime Control and Safe Streets Act of 1968, and the District of Columbia Crime and Criminal Procedure Act of 1967, the subsequent attempts to overrule the Court, particularly in regard to its more recently developed policies regarding reapportionment and religious freedom, have taken the form of proposed constitutional amendments; and except for one section (that the Senate rejected) of the omnibus crime bill, they have been presented as assaults upon the issues rather than upon the Court. We shall consider them presently when we turn to the reactions to the Court's particular policies.

The best-known modern example of presidential reaction to the Supreme Court's decisions is of course that of Franklin Roosevelt in 1937. It is enough for present purposes to remark that Roosevelt was beaten in Congress; and evidently he was beaten at his own game of taking the issue directly to the public (through "fireside" radio addresses and other propaganda efforts) because the available data (admittedly crude early Gallup polls) show that he never had majority support, and was slipping badly by the end of spring.[47] But he did beat the Hughes Court; he packed it, and he reformed it, and the Court has never been the same since.

Harry Truman was challenged by the Supreme Court's decision in the Steel Seizure case; but he had vowed in advance of the decision to accept it, and did so. Eisenhower was not so much challenged personally by the Court (as his two immediate predecessors had been) as he was challenged to *do* something, by events that stemmed directly from the Southern counterattack against the Court's school desegregation decision. But when forced to act, as he finally was by the confrontation at Little Rock, Eisenhower backed up the Court with troops, a precedent that John F. Kennedy felt obliged to follow five years later in order to assure James Meredith's admission to the University of Mississippi. During the congressional campaign against the Warren Court, however, Eisenhower remained more or less personally, and strictly officially, neutral, exploiting his status as just a confused layman, and leaving his subordinates to walk both sides of the congressional street, as many of them did.[48]

One further aspect of interaction between the Court and the regime is that of the justices' own responses to the feedback that they receive from the various external constraints that we have been considering. Law reviews, for example, are a source of persuasion as well as of enlightenment; and their general thrust—at least, in comparison with most alternative legal sources—is liberal and toward legal change. In more conservative legal cultures, such as the Canadian, it is considered to be pretty audacious for a judge (or an attorney!) to cite a law journal article. Newland has shown that there was a sharp and steady increase in such references in the opinions of United States Supreme Court justices, beginning in 1939. The Four Horsemen of the Hughes Court "cited practically no law review writing." The justices who most conspicuously did cite them, up through a decade ago when the study upon which I am relying was published,[49] were Frankfurter, Douglas, Rutledge, and Stone—all former law professors. Frankfurter demonstrated that these sort of legal references could be used to subserve conservative as well as liberal policy goals. A closely related example of feedback of an even more complicated nature is provided by Anthony Lewis, the former but esteemed reporter specialist on the Court, for the *New York Times*. While back at Harvard during 1956–1957 as a Nieman Fellow at the Law School, Lewis wrote an article[50] that presents the basic policy goals and arguments that are incorporated in the brief submitted for the government by Solicitor General Cox,[51] which in turn reappears in the majority opinion in *Baker* v. *Carr*.[52]

But we need not feel confined to opinions for examples of judicial response to feedback from the regime to the Court. Clearly, the voting behavior of Roberts in 1937, and of Frankfurter in 1959, both represent attempts to adapt homeopathically to a threatening environment. It was not, in either instance, a foolproof strategy, as was demonstrated when Hughes forced Roberts and the three liberals into dissent as late in the spring as May 24, 1937;[53] and again, when Harlan joined with the four liberals of the Warren Court on June 1, 1959, to reverse a federal loyalty dismissal [54]—an outcome that hardly meshed well with Frankfurter's plans for the other (and negative) political freedom decisions that came later that month, marking the inception of the Warren Court's civil liberties recession. Of course, Warren himself "refused to retreat." [55] The rift between Frankfurter and the chief justice had become an open one by 1957; and as Walter Murphy has pointed out, Warren did not assign Frankfurter to write for the Court in any of the major political freedom cases of that term, although Frankfurter voted with the liberal majority in six of the seven decisions.[56] As the senior associate voting with the majority in the withdrawal action at the end of the following term, it became Frankfurter's turn to assign, as he did, the opinion of the Court in *Uphaus* to Clark, the author of the dissenting opinions in the counterparts of 1957, *Sweezy* and *Watkins*.[57] These internal maneuverings, I suggest, were the consequences of differing appraisals of where the better part of wisdom, as well as of valor, lay in the face of the developing storm over those decisions of 1957.

What Has Been the Impact of the Warren Court's Policies?

In the concluding part of this volume I shall attempt to evaluate what is the most difficult aspect of the Court's work to appraise precisely: the effect that the Court's policies have had upon the persons and groups whose behavior they were intended to influence. The subject is difficult primarily because of the very limited amount of research that has been done. It is one thing to suggest heuristic paradigms with arrows labeled "impact" and "feedback"; it is quite another matter to design, attract support for, and carry out the needed empirical inquiries. It is my hope that the following brief sketch will not only summarize what little we know that is relevant about the social impact of the Warren Court's major decisions, but that it may also direct attention to the kind of judicial process research that badly needs further development.

By way of introduction, let us examine what the survey research evidence shows to have been the degrees of public awareness of, and of opposition to, the Court's major policies, in the mid-sixties.[58] Over a third named racial equality as a Court issue in 1964, and almost a third specified religious freedom. However, nine out of ten could indicate like or dislike for the Court's policy on racial equality, while only half could do this for religious freedom. Only one person in twenty selected either fair procedure or voting equality as a Court issue; and political freedom—the core issue of McCarthyism, and of the congressional backlash against the Court only half a dozen years earlier—had become so invisible to the American public that it is subsumed in the research report, along with privacy and civic equality, under the catchall rubric of "other responses," for both the 1964 and the 1966 surveys. Of those few respondents who named fair procedure as an issue in 1964, only 11 per cent agreed with the Court, although 38 per cent of the equivalently small number of respondents who were aware of the Court's reapportionment policy claimed to agree with it. What these findings show is that only small minorities of the populace knew anything about the Court's decisions affecting either criminal trials or reapportionment; and that among these discrete minorities sentiment against the Court ranged from preponderant to overwhelming for three of what were perceived to be the four major Court issues; and even on the issue of racial equality, majority sentiment was against the Court. (To what extent the majorities were all negative, because the question asked first for dislikes and then for likes,[59] we can only speculate.)

It should be noted, too, that the 1964 survey came less than six months after the Court's decision in a score of major cases affecting the legislatures of fifteen states,[60] when mass media publicity about reapportionment was relatively very high; and that this was a postelection survey of a presidential campaign during which the Republican candidate had tried hard to focus national attention upon the dangerous errors in the Supreme Court's policies, explicitly in regard to reapportionment, fair procedure, and religious freedom. It seems clear that Goldwater was not getting through any better than the Court itself. Moreover, within two years public awareness of reapportionment had dropped to less than one person in a hundred; and even concern for what the Court was doing in regard to racial equality and religious freedom had fallen off, in each instance to about one person in four. The only issue for which awareness increased was fair procedure, which rose from 6 per cent in 1964 to 16 per cent in 1966, and which became the subject of anti-Court legislation by Congress twice in a period of less than six months beginning December 27, 1967. It seems pretty clear what it *did* take to bring about this moderate increase in concern for the Court's policies affecting law and order: the riots that broke out, beginning in August 1965 in Watts, in the major urban centers *outside of* the South. It is also true but it is probably coincidental that by 1966, fair procedure was the cutting edge and the emphasis in the Court's work had moved away from reapportionment, religious freedom, and even racial equality except as that became merged with fair procedure issues in decisions relating to group protests and civil rights demonstrations in the form of marches and sit-ins.

The periodic Gallup polls, beginning in the summer of 1954, indicated continuing approval by a clear majority of the public for the Court's school desegregation policy,[61] with no apparent partisan difference outside of the South.[62] On the other hand, in interpreting these data, we should keep in mind not only the differences in theory, technique, and goals as between the Gallup organization and the Survey Research Center; and not only the halo effect, previously mentioned, that comes from asking people to give an opinion on a subject concerning which they have no opinion; but also the catalytic effect, upon recall, of suggesting issues to respondents instead of asking them to suggest issues to interviewers. In August 1964, for example, 77 per cent of Gallup's sample had an opinion about legislative reapportionment, and of these 61 per cent favored it; but only three months later the Survey Research Center reported an opposite division with 62 per cent *opposed,* from among the less than 5 per cent of the sample who indicated awareness of the issue.[63] It may well be prudent, therefore, to read through dark glasses the enthusiastic reports that emanated from Princeton concerning majority national support for racial equality.

It is important, also, to keep in mind that public opinion, as a response to the Court, must be distinguished from individual and group political activity as a response to the Court. In this regard, Martin Shapiro has suggested in correspondence to me that public opinion is not a static concept but a series of questions about shifting balances of support and opposition at various levels of knowledge, which are themselves functions of both real world changes and changes that result from the sociopsychological dynamics of the evolving political controversy. The crucial question in regard to the Court, says Shapiro, is not what people know or believe in some abstract and static sense, but rather it is who would be prepared and able to act on such knowledge, and how. Of course such research is not available for me to draw upon at this time, but I do think Shapiro is correct in arguing that future work on mass attitudes toward the Court ought to seek a level of analysis more sophisticated and complex than the simple stratification of general public opinion among socioeconomic and political identification variables. The latter is both relevant and important, but it is only a first step.

According to Mitau, by 1962 over a fourth of the school districts in the southern and border states were formally desegregated, although less than a fourth *of one per cent* of the Negro school children in that region actually were attending classes with whites.[64] That proportion had been increased to 6 per cent by 1965, of which half had begun to do so only in the previous year—a full decade after the Supreme Court's decision in *Brown* v. *Board of Education* —and there were still three states (Alabama, Mississippi, and Louisiana) in which the ratio remained less than one per cent. In Prince Edward County, Virginia, whose school board had been one of the original defendants in *Brown*, the percentage remained at zero: total segregation. But part of the belated response to the *Brown* decision, and one that no doubt is attributable primarily to such intervening political responses as the March on Washington in August 1963, was the enactment of the Civil Rights Act of 1964, part of which provided for a system of administrative implementation of school desegregation by withholding federal money; and within another three years this system was upheld by decisions of both the Fifth Circuit U.S. Court of Appeals, and the Supreme Court itself. Whether one will consider this kind and degree of compliance with *Brown* to be substantial or not will depend, no doubt, upon one's hopes, expectations, and judgment concerning the limits of feasibility. Moreover, it should be noted that what liberals call "de facto school segregation," [65] resulting primarily as the by-product of residential segregation, is increasing in metropolitan areas outside the South, perhaps as rapidly as de jure school desegregation has been proceeding within the South.[66] And whether the Supreme Court will decide that its policy of school desegregation extends to require school integration remains an open question.

Nineteen-sixty marked the beginning of direct political, social, and economic action, on a widespread basis, to force greater acceptance of the policy of racial equality on an across-the-board basis. Protests against racial discrimination since then have become increasingly common and effective, reaching an at least temporary climax of sorts in the encampment known as Resurrection City, in Washington during the summer of 1968.[67] These demonstrations also can be seen as action that intervened between the Court's decisions and the response of Congress in the public accommodations section of the Civil Rights Act of 1964; similarly, the Freedom March from Selma to Montgomery in March 1965 bridged the gap between the Court's white primary decision of 1944 and the Voting Rights Act of 1965. But SNCC and CORE and Black Panthers also are among the consequences of *Brown* v. *Board of Education*;[68] and so part of the impact of the Supreme Court's policy of racial equality, intended to eliminate racial segregation from the American way of life, has become a drive for black apartheid which is the very antithesis of the liberal ethic that motivated the Warren Court.

Notwithstanding the publicity that it received, the question of religion in the public schools has in practice proved to be a much easier problem to handle, both for the Court and for the country. It has also proved to be more manageable to study, from the point of view of impact analysis. There is even available that rare enterprise in social research, a pair of surveys that were carried out before and after the event under investigation.

A decade ago, there were a dozen states—a majority in the South, and the rest in the northeast, except for Idaho— which required Bible reading in their public schools. Thirty-one other states permitted Bible reading or school prayers, mostly by local option. Only the remaining seven states forbade school religious exercises on grounds of state constitutional policy. Bible reading was least common in communities with a population of less than 2,500.[69] A later study reported that in 1963 there were eighteen states, half in the South, that had explicit constitutional or statutory provisions requiring or permitting daily Bible reading.[70]

The Supreme Court's major decisions came as a one-two punch, with disapproval of school prayers in 1962 and disapproval of Bible reading the following year. The elite reaction in response to the initial decision came quickly; it was attacked by the incumbent president of the ABA the day after it was announced. Several state chief justices followed suit, and so did the litterateurs of the law schools, such as Harvard's Mark De Wolfe Howe. The American Roman Catholic cardinals joined with Billy Graham in denouncing the Court. President John F. Kennedy was one of the few defenders of the Court who could and did command a national audience; the press failed to use the remarks of even such prominent speakers as Arthur Goldberg, then still secretary of labor but soon to join the Court, whose speech on the subject was reported only locally, in a single paper. Similarly overlooked was a speech by Justice Clark at the ABA convention that summer. We can, of course, assume that in highlighting the attack on the Court, and ignoring whatever rational justification might be offered in the Court's defense, the American press was not showing bias, but, rather in the spirit of fair play and public service that customarily motivates it, was merely trying to peddle its papers. It is true, nonetheless, that editorial sentiment was split almost two-to-one (63 per cent) against the Court, according to a survey made following the initial decision, in the school prayer case.[71] A subsequent, differently designed, and quite independent study of editorial reaction in a single local community confirmed that the press there also published editorial material and syndicated columns that were 64 per cent opposed to the school prayer decision. However, this later survey showed a vast swing in sentiment concerning the Bible-reading decision of 1963, with only half as much published and only 17 per cent of that critical.[72] This same study examined the output of the three leading national news magazines for both years, and again found that over twice as much coverage was given to *Engel* in 1962 as to *Schempp* in 1963.[73] As for the religious press, "the conservative and Catholic journals found themselves in opposition, while the liberal and protestant ones generally supported the Court in both cases." [74]

In 1964, the year after *Schempp* was announced, a group of over a hundred congressmen, mostly Republicans or Southern Democrats, introduced a large number of proposed constitutional amendments, under the leadership of Representative Frank Becker of New York. Most major Protestant and Jewish groups voiced opposition, as did also some 223 leading constitutional lawyers; but the fundamentalist churches, Cardinal Spellman, and the dean of the Harvard Law School all supported the Becker Resolution. Opinion was sufficiently divided both within the House and within the country that the measure was buried in the Judiciary Committee by Chairman Emanuel Celler; and a discharge petition fell far short of a majority. Senate Minority Leader Dirksen then substituted a more restricted provision, authorizing prayer but not Bible reading, for a UNICEF resolution that happened to be available. The Dirksen Prayer Amendment, as it was called, came to a vote in September

1966; and although it attracted the support of a clear majority, it fell short of the two-thirds needed for adoption by the Senate. On two measures of ideology that were applied to examine the roll call, three-fourths of the supporters of the Dirksen Resolution were strong conservatives, while all except three or four of those who opposed it were staunch liberals.[75]

Further evidence bearing upon compliance with *Schempp* is found in the response of the lower, and particularly of the state, courts. In sharp contrast to the racial segregation issue, all except one state court backed up the Supreme Court on religious freedom. The exception came from Florida, and was reversed summarily by the Warren Court.[76]

Frank Way has reported a survey of a national random sample of over two thousand public elementary school teachers.[77] Way's study showed that 61 per cent of his respondents had conducted morning-prayer exercises, and 48 per cent Bible readings, before the Court's decision; but by the time of the survey in 1964–1965, these proportions had dropped to 24 per cent and 22 per cent, respectively. This would suggest that there had been a substantial decrease in school religious exercises, as a consequence of the Court's intervening decisions. However, Way's data also show that released time programs were being carried on in about a quarter of the schools with which these respondents were associated, and that 15 per cent of these programs were being carried out on the school premises, directly contrary to the Court's policy as announced in 1948, over sixteen years earlier. Over 60 per cent of the respondents said that their schools had no policy on either prayers or Bible reading, leaving such matters up to the teacher's discretion; only 31 per cent had a policy forbidding either type of religious exercise, in compliance with the Court's decisions; and a minority of about 8 per cent retained formal policies requiring prayers or Bible reading or both, the Supreme Court to the contrary notwithstanding. The parallelism in school policies, regarding the two types of exercises, was not accompanied by a similar equivalence in classroom practices, however. The Bible was read in 91 per cent of the schools that required this, but in only 25 per cent of the schools that left it up to the teacher, and in only 3 per cent of those where it was against school policy. Prayers were said in 43 per cent of the schools that so required, and in almost as many (40 per cent) where it was left to the teacher's discretion, but only in 4 per cent of the schools that forbade it. Clearly, teachers throughout the country were following a combination of the policies laid down by the local school authorities plus their own predilections rather than what the Supreme Court said the Constitution required.[78] Probably the major effect of the Court's decisions was to shift the formal policies of a substantial minority of the local schools out of the category of mandating the religious exercises, and into the category of permitting them by having no uniform or formal policy. Way did find "that once the Court decisions were announced the Roman Catholic and Jewish teachers were more willing to accept a ban on classroom religious practices than were Protestant teachers." [79] He also found that when his data were ordered by national regions, the South was very different from the rest of the country: "In the responses to five out of six opinion questions about religion in the public school the South was the most conservative area. . . . Both before and after the Supreme Court decisions prayers and Bible-reading were more likely to occur in Southern classrooms than elsewhere in the nation." [80] Bible reading was still required by school policy in 23 per cent of the schools in the South, and in only 1 per cent elsewhere; it was explicitly prohibited in only 11 per cent of the southern schools, but by 42 per cent in the rest of the country. In four northeastern states (Maine, Massachusetts, New Jersey, and Pennsylvania) Bible reading was practiced in 96 per cent of the relevant respondents' classrooms before *Schempp,* but it was no longer practiced in 97 per cent of these same classrooms by the time of this survey.[81]

These findings about southern noncompliance with the Court's policy of religious freedom are confirmed by the before-and-after study, which showed that in 1960, Bible reading was conducted in 42 per cent of the nation's public elementary classrooms, ranging from a high of 77 per cent in the South and 68 per cent in the East to 18 per cent in the Midwest and only 11 per cent in the West.[82] The corresponding proportions in 1966 were down to 14 per cent for the nation, with the South still 52 per cent, and the rest of the country 5 per cent or less. Compliance was almost perfectly negatively correlated with population density, and was least (70 per cent) for urban areas with populations of over 100,000, ranging upwards to a high of 91 per cent in rural communities under 2,500 (like the locus of Richard Johnson's case study of a midwestern rural school district.)

Johnson emphasized the importance of the roles of both school personnel, and of civic leaders whom he calls "influentials," in structuring acquiescence by the rest of the district in what was generally perceived by them to be the Supreme Court's "Godless" policies. Johnson's data show that approximately half of each of the three classes of participants were personally in disagreement with the Court; the precise ratios are 49 per cent for the educators, 47 per cent for the influentials, and 57 per cent for the rest of the community. Where they critically differed, however, was in regard to agreement as distinguished from fence sitting: 46 per cent of the educators, and 44 per cent of the influentials approved of the Court's policy; and although only

12 per cent of the rest (and by far, of course, the bulk) of the community approved, almost a third of them (31 per cent) were undecided.[83] Evidently, these latter were the persons who could be and were led by the community elite who both made the decision to acquiesce and were in a position to carry it out. Johnson asked his respondents how they felt about the duty to comply with the Court's decisions, irrespective of one's personal beliefs; and he was then able to measure the relation between agreeing privately with the Court's policy, and asserting that the Court's policy ought to be carried out. The correlation was $+.52$; and if one can assume that the 4 persons (out of a sample of 159) who said that the Court ought to be disobeyed, even though they personally agreed with the Court on the merits of the school-religion issue, were confused, and are examples of the kind of empirical error variance that one expects to find in survey work, then there is the appropriate zero cell to indicate a scale relation between the two attitudes, with the public attitude toward compliance dominating the private attitude toward the policy issue. Thus understood, the critical decision makers in this community, on this issue, were not the majority who were either both against Bible reading and for compliance, or else for Bible reading and against compliance. The critical people were rather those who were cross pressured, privately disagreeing with but publicly upholding the Court's policy.[84] And these thirty individuals were drawn in equal proportions from the ranks of the school personnel, the influentials, and the others.

In the social and political context of civil rights protests and demonstrations in the South and race riots in the urban areas elsewhere, plus the publicity attracted by the presidential campaigns of Barry Goldwater and George Wallace, the issue of law and order assured a mixed reception to the Court's still-unfolding policy of fair procedure

for indigent criminal defendants. The best publicized of
these decisions—*Gideon, Escobedo,* and *Miranda*—came in
1963, 1964, and 1966. Congressional reaction was predominantly hostile, like public opinion which (according to
the Harris poll in November 1966) was 2–1 against the
Court.[85] After the defeat of the anti-*Mallory* and related
crime control bills in 1959, the focus of efforts toward legislative reform of what was perceived to be the Court's misguided policy shifted to the District of Columbia, increasingly a crime-gutted area in which congressmen had to work
and through which they had to travel. First an omnibus
crime bill for the district, and then one for the rest of the
country, were enacted during the 1967–1968 session, purporting to overrule in part *Mallory* and *Miranda,* and also a
more recent decision in which the Court had extended to
police line-ups the right to counsel.[86] The new acts posited
for federal criminal trials rules of procedure designed to enhance the admissibility of confessions and to extend the time
for police interrogation after arrest (and also, incidentally, to
relax restrictions on wiretapping while tightening up the
control over obscenity in the District).

During 1964, the year following the Court's decision in
Gideon, over fifty similar appeals came to the Court from
a dozen other states; and in Florida (the source of Gideon's
own appeal) alone, over a thousand prisoners were released, and over 70 per cent of three hundred others who
had been granted new trials received reduced sentences, because their original convictions had been without the assistance of counsel as *Gideon* required. Within two years
half of the states had enacted legislation or revised their
judicial policies in an attempt to comply with the Court's
new line.[87] It soon appeared, however, that both fiscal and
administrative problems of no little complexity had been
posed by the Court's empty-handed munificence. As recently

as a year or two ago, there were still no organized systems
—public or private—for providing counsel for indigent defendants in 2900 of the 3100 counties in the country. Less
than five years ago there were only 136 public defender's
offices in the United States, and Congress refused to include
a public defender system in the Criminal Justice Act of
1964, which establishes local option for federal district
courts as between assigned counsel and private legal aid.[88]

Abraham Blumberg, a participant-observer in the process
and a criminal lawyer with a doctorate in sociology, has
proffered the discouraging prognosis that "recent Supreme
Court decisions may have a long range effect which is
radically different from that intended or anticipated. The
more libertarian rules will tend to produce the rather ironic
end result of augmenting the *existing* organizational arrangements, enriching court organizations with more personnel
and elaborate structure, which in turn will maximize organizational goals of 'efficiency' and production. Thus, many
defendants will find that courts will possess an even more
sophisticated apparatus for processing them toward a guilty
plea!" [89] He claims that municipal courts function as a
bureaucratic system geared towards conviction,[90] irrespective
whether the mandated defense be from among the specialized criminal bar[91] or from among the vast majority of
the local bar who are equally untrained and uninterested
in defending indigents, particularly when co-opted to do
so without fee, or with only a nominal one. His recent study
reports that by the time of the second contact with the
defendant, four-fifths of the lawyers (irrespective of the
style of their employment) advised their clients to cop out.
(The precise ratios are: by assigned counsel, 77 per cent;
by legal aid counsel, 78 per cent; and by privately retained
counsel, 79 per cent.)[92] There is apparently a substantial
gap here, between the Court's "Thou shalts" and the trau-

matic changes, in the organization and in the functioning of the legal profession, that would be required to transform the ideals posited by the Court into an attainable, let alone a proximate, reality.

In the light of the compliance record on reapportionment —which is by far the best for any of the issues that we have considered—it is ironic to recall that two-thirds of the respondents who had views on the subject, in the 1964 national survey by the Survey Research Center, said they disagreed with the Court. It is necessary to recall, however, that those with views comprised less than 5 per cent of this sample, and less than 1 per cent of the follow-up survey two years later. This was, in short, the kind of issue regarding which political elites were free to act almost without concern for what public opinion might be—because for all practical purposes, there was no public opinion about reapportionment.

Newspaper commentary was overwhelmingly favorable to the Court, but only about 10 per cent of those papers examined in a national survey bothered to mention reapportionment at all.[93] Those really concerned about the issue were the political professionals in the state legislatures and in the Congress; and for a very good reason: they were the ones directly involved. What the Court's policy really accomplished was to encourage and expedite change that benefited both parties in (and within) the states where they were weakest, and for this reason it was a policy that could and did attract bipartisan support, on the whole, throughout the country. Typical of the congressmen beaten within their own parties, in primary elections in 1966 following state redistricting decisions, were Democrat Howard Smith of Virginia and Republican Joseph Martin of Massachusetts; but these were the kind of long-overdue losses that very few persons could be induced to lament.

The state legislative establishment proposed, through its organ the Council of State Governments, that the Supreme Court be given a governess in the form of a new "Court of the Union," to consist of the fifty state chief justices. This is a fascinating and creative proposal, one which I suppose I would have to oppose, if it ever came to that, but toward which my private attitude (for entirely selfish academic reasons) is not all that hostile. Congress ignored such foolishness, but the House did pass in 1964 the Tuck Bill, which would have precluded federal courts from exercising jurisdiction in regard to state legislative reapportionment; the Senate defeated the bill by a large majority. Attention then shifted to the Dirksen Resolution, a proposed constitutional amendment which was defeated in August 1965 and again in 1966, both times with a conservative coalition majority that was strong but seven votes short of the necessary two-thirds plurality.[94]

In the meantime the state legislatures had been proceeding to comply with the Court's policy. Sixty per cent had reapportioned both houses by 1966, and most of the others had reapportioned whichever house was the more seriously out of line with the Court's standard. Judicial compliance in the federal lower courts was high,[95] and this was, in any event, a battle that was fought out strictly between lawyers and in judicial chambers—not in the streets.

There is, of course, no simple and clear-cut answer that applies across the board to the question: what has been the impact of the Warren Court's policies? Some issues that loomed large only a decade ago, such as political freedom for the Marxist left, have been displaced; other aspects of political freedom relating to censorship of communication in art and literature remain viable but do not appear to have been adequately studied to permit appraisal from the point of view of compliance, although the evidence available does indicate that in the movie censorship board or in the book-shop, what counts most is not what the Supreme Court says about prurience but rather it is a combination of the personal tastes of the censor or shopkeeper plus his own assessment of the balance of competing interests in his own community.[96] Moreover, it does seem indisputable that the Supreme Court's generally liberal policy thrust—notwith-standing some vacillation and ambiguity—in the direction of greater freedom of communication in the purveyance of paperbacks and movies has paralleled (if it has not evoked) a quite dramatic proletarian response in matters of sex (or the lack thereof), sadism, bestiality, speech, dress/undress, coiffeur, and narcotism, in both public and private deport-ment, as well as in music, drama, art, literature, and in what must by any conventional standard be deemed pornography. But the Court's impact has not yet been adequately meas-ured; and the behavioral changes noted—which appear, in-cidentally, to be quite global in their scope—can hardly be attributed exclusively, and probably not even primarily, to the influence of the Court. Other issues such as the right to privacy, and to civic equality, have not yet emerged (ex-cept among small elites) as significant questions for political debate; there has been no compliance problem, in recent years, concerning any of these. As for the remaining four, we have found that reapportionment was quickly and widely accepted, both as a policy norm and in practice; and that except in the South, the Court's religious freedom policy purportedly has been accepted in practice if not in principle. The remaining two issues pose much larger difficulties. There remains widespread popular disagreement, in principle, with the fair procedure policy. What will be the practical result of either a program of legicare or, if the socialization of legal services in any serious way seems improbable, then of reorganizing legal training and practice in the revolutionary mode that will be necessary before reliance upon noblesse oblige will prove to be more of a cure than a curse? Nobody knows, and least of all, the Supreme Court. Such technical questions aside, the odds under present political conditions favor a recession in favor of more law and order, and away from the ideals posited by the Warren Court. Concerning racial equality, disagreement in principle with the Court's norms is largely confined to radical minorities of both the left and the right, but the political problems of social reconstruction are many and complex, and their solutions (if there are solutions) are unlikely to be aided by violence and revolution. The Warren Court could and did force the issue in its first major policy decision; but how the issue would be resolved is a question that no one could answer, even a decade and a half later, as the Warren Court era ended.

Both the Supreme Court and the nation have come a long way since 1921. During this half century, there have been great changes in the presidency and in national administration—though not so many in Congress; but even greater changes have occurred in the constitutional role of the Court. From the chief symbol and protector of the interests of men of property, the Court has become the friend of the poor, the downtrodden, the social and the political outcast. Formerly the third and most conservative chamber of the national legislature, the Court now has become the superego of the American polity, goading and prodding the Congress and the presidency, and the states and their localities, into programs and policies of social and political reform. It is perhaps remarkable that such a change in role should have resulted from strictly incremental (and by no means consistent) changes in the composition of a small group of elderly and politically irresponsible lawyers. Certainly there was nothing in the constraints imposed by the regime that compelled the Court to make the choices that it did. But neither did the regime preclude the Court's assuming a libertarian role; and the political system's continuing restriction of the presidency, throughout the forty years from 1928 to 1968, to men who represented the moderate to the somewhat left-of-center factions within their respective political parties—and all of the really conservative options were rejected until Nixon's election in 1968—shaped the Court with the constellation of values that has become increasingly dominant during the past two decades.

As Earl Warren has said, the justices are not spectators of American political life; they are instead among its creators. They are caught up, as he put it, in the living stream of our national development. Under Warren's leadership, in particular, the Supreme Court has been riding—like the rest of us—on the crest of the torrents of spring.

NOTES

Chapter I. Constitutional Policy

1. "Plus ça change, plus c'est la même chose."
2. Bertrand Russell, "A Free Man's Worship" (originally published in 1903; reprinted in his *Mysticism and Logic* [New York: W. W. Norton, 1918]).
3. Cf. Harry Woolf, ed., *Quantification: A History of the Meaning of Measurement in the Natural and Social Sciences* (Indianapolis: Bobbs-Merrill, 1961).
4. See my "Behavioral Jurisprudence," *Law and Society Review* 2 (1968): 407–28.
5. See my "The Rhetoric of Constitutional Change," *Journal of Public Law* 16 (1967): 16–50.
6. *E.g.*, John D. Sprague, *Voting Patterns of the United States Supreme Court: Cases in Federalism, 1889–1959* (Indianapolis: Bobbs-Merrill, 1968), especially Ch. 4; Eloise C. Snyder, "The Supreme Court as a Small Group," *Social Forces* 36 (1958): 232–38.
7. Arnold M. Paul, *Conservative Crisis and the Rule of Law: Attitudes of Bar and Bench, 1887–1895* (Ithaca: Cornell University Press, 1960).
8. Walton H. Hamilton, "The Path of Due Process of Law," in Conyers Read, ed., *The Constitution Reconsidered* (New York: Columbia University Press, 1938), pp. 168–90.
9. *Pollock v. Farmers' Loan and Trust Company*, 157 U.S. 429, 607 (1895).
10. *Dred Scott v. Sandford*, 19 How. 393, 403 (1857).
11. *Plessy v. Ferguson*, 163 U.S. 537, 551–552 (1896).
12. Alan F. Westin, "John Marshall Harlan," in Allison Dunham and Philip B. Kurland, eds., *Mr. Justice* (Chicago: University of Chicago, 1964), pp. 93–128.
13. *Plessy v. Ferguson*, 163 U.S. 537, 559 (1896).

14. Charles Fairman, "The Retirement of Federal Judges," *Harvard Law Review* 51 (1938): 397–443; David J. Danelski, "A Supreme Court Justice Steps Down," *Yale Review* 54 (1965): 411–12.

15. Alfred H. Kelly and Winfred A. Harbison, *The American Constitution: Its Origins and Development* (New York: Norton, 1948), p. 552.

16. Holmes, in *Schenck* v. *United States,* 249 U.S. 47, 52 (1919).

17. *Buck* v. *Bell,* 274 U.S. 200, 207 (1927). Cf. Julius Paul, "The Return of Punitive Sterilization Proposals: Current Attacks on Illegitimacy and the AFDC Program," *Law and Society Review* 3 (1968): 77–106.

18. *Prudential Insurance Co. of America* v. *Cheek,* 259 U.S. 530, 543 (1922).

19. See my *Constitutional Politics: The Political Behavior of Supreme Court Justices and the Constitutional Policies that They Make* (New York: Holt, Rinehart and Winston, 1960), p. 335.

20. Alpheus T. Mason, *Bureaucracy Convicts Itself* (New York: Viking, 1941); Winifred McCulloch, "The Glavis-Ballinger Dispute" in Harold Stein, ed., *Public Administration and Policy Development* (New York: Harcourt, Brace, 1952), pp. 77–87.

21. *Near* v. *Minnesota,* 283 U.S. 697, 707 (1931).

22. See my *The Presidency in the Courts* (Minneapolis: University of Minnesota Press, 1957), Ch. 2.

23. See James Hart, *The American Presidency in Action: 1789* (New York: Macmillan, 1948); Leonard D. White, *The Federalists* (New York: Macmillan, 1948).

24. *Adkins* v. *Children's Hospital,* 261 U.S. 525 (1923); *Morehead* v. *Tipaldo,* 298 U.S. 587 (1936).

25. Schubert, *Constitutional Politics,* pp. 168–70.

26. C. Herman Pritchett, *The Roosevelt Court: A Study in Judicial Politics and Values, 1937–1947* (New York: Macmillan, 1948), p. 25.

27. 295 U.S. 441 (1935).

28. 301 U.S. 242 (1937).

29. Arthur S. Miller, *The Supreme Court and American Capitalism* (New York: The Free Press, 1968), p. 199.

30. Ibid., pp. 93, 103.

31. Martin Shapiro, *Law and Politics in the Supreme Court: New Approaches to Political Jurisprudence* (New York: The Free Press, 1964), Ch. 6; Schubert, *Constitutional Politics,* pp. 244–51: "Professional and Judicial Sports."

NOTES

32. Martin Shapiro, *The Supreme Court and Administrative Agencies* (New York: Macmillan, 1968), pp. 145, 222–23.

33. *Constitutional Politics*, pp. 240, 242.

34. *Roosevelt Court*, p. 190.

35. Joseph Tanenhaus, "Supreme Court Attitudes toward Federal Administrative Agencies, 1947–1956—An Application of Social Science Methods to the Study of the Judicial Process," *Vanderbilt Law Review* 14 (1961): 473–502, Table 2.

36. Harold J. Spaeth, "Warren Court Attitudes toward Business: The 'B' Scale," in Glendon Schubert, ed., *Judicial Decision-Making* (New York: The Free Press of Glencoe, 1963), p. 90.

37. Harold J. Spaeth, *The Warren Court: Cases and Commentary* (San Francisco: Chandler, 1966), p. 35.

38. *Supreme Court and Administrative Agencies*, p. 264.

39. Walter Gellhorn and Clark Byse, *Administrative Law: Cases and Comments* (Brooklyn: Foundation Press, 1954 ed.), p. 641.

40. *Jones v. Securities and Exchange Commission*, 298 U.S. 1 (1936).

41. Gellhorn and Byse, *Administrative Law*, p. 61, n. 48.

42. *Supreme Court and Administrative Agencies*, p. 266.

43. See my *The Judicial Mind: Attitudes and Ideologies of Supreme Court Justices, 1946–1963* (Evanston: Northwestern University Press, 1965), p. 170.

44. *Roosevelt Court*, p. 257.

45. "Supreme Court Attitudes," Tables 4-A and 4-B.

46. "Warren Court Attitudes," p. 90; *Warren Court*, pp. 35, 56.

47. Alan Westin, *The Anatomy of a Constitutional Law Case* (New York: Macmillan, 1958); Grant McConnell, *The Steel Seizure of 1952* (University, Alabama: University of Alabama Press, 1958).

48. *Roosevelt Court*, p. 257.

49. "Warren Court Attitudes," pp. 92–94.

50. *Roosevelt Court*, pp. 208, 224–28.

51. Harold J. Spaeth, "An Analysis of Judicial Attitudes in the Labor Relations Decisions of the Warren Court," *Journal of Politics* 25 (1963): 299–304.

52. "Supreme Court Attitudes," Table 4-B.

53. "Warren Court Attitudes," p. 96.

54. "Supreme Court Attitudes," Table 4-A.

55. "Analysis of Judicial Attitudes," p. 303.

56. *Roosevelt Court*, pp. 190–91.

57. "Warren Court Attitudes," pp. 99–100.

58. *Judicial Mind*, pp. 161–63.

59. This finding is supported by the analysis in Martin Shapiro, "The Warren Court and the Interstate Commerce Commission," *Stanford Law Review* 18 (1965): 112–16.

60. *First Iowa Hydro-Electric Cooperative* v. *Federal Power Commission*, 328 U.S. 152 (1946).

61. See my "Policy without Law: An Extension of the Certiorari Game," *Stanford Law Review* 14 (1962): 284–327.

62. Spaeth, *Warren Court*, p. 355.

63. *Supreme Court and American Capitalism*, pp. 79–80; *Morey* v. *Doud*, 354 U.S. 457 (1957).

64. *Grigg* v. *Allegheny Co.*, 369 U.S. 84 (1962).

65. *Schroeder* v. *City of New York*, 371 U.S. 208 (1962).

66. *Department of Employment* v. *United States* 385 U.S. 355 (1966).

67. Pritchett, *Roosevelt Court*, p. 89.

68. But cf. *Polar Ice Cream* v. *Andrew*, 375 U.S. 361 (1963), an unanimous decision by the Warren Court.

69. *Southern Pacific Co.* v. *Arizona*, 325 U.S. 761 (1945); but cf. *Brotherhood of Locomotive Firemen* v. *Chicago, Rock Island & Pacific R.R.*, 393 U.S. 129 (1968).

70. *Hostetter* v. *Idlewild*, 377 U.S. 324 (1964); *Department of Revenue* v. *Beam*, 377 U.S. 341 (1964).

71. *Warren Court*, pp. 34–35.

72. Pritchett, *Roosevelt Court*, p. 257; Schubert, *Judicial Mind*, p. 148; Spaeth, *Warren Court*, p. 18.

73. Herbert Stroup, *The Jehovah's Witnesses* (New York: Columbia University Press, 1945); David Manwaring, *Render unto Caesar: The Flag Salute Controversy* (Chicago: University of Chicago Press, 1962); Clement E. Vose, "Litigation as a Form of Pressure Group Activity," *Annals of the American Academy of Political and Social Science* 319 (1958): 22.

74. Schubert, *Constitutional Politics*, pp. 239–41.

75. Cf. the oral testimony of Professor Martin Shapiro, at the *Hearings before the [Ervin] Subcommittee on the Separation of Powers of the Committee on the Judiciary*, U.S. Senate, 90th Cong., 2nd sess. on the Supreme Court (June 11, 12, 13, 14, 1968), pp. 173–78.

76. See Samuel Krislov, *The Supreme Court and Political Freedom* (New York: The Free Press, 1968), pp. 42–48, for a review of some of the evidence.

77. *Brown* v. *Board of Education*, 347 U.S. 483, 492–93 (1954).

78. *Olmstead* v. *United States*, 277 U.S. 438, 478 (1928).

79. *Schmerber* v. *California*, 384 U.S. 757, 759 (1966).

80. For a survey of the issues, arguments, and short-run effects, see Gordon E. Baker, *The Reapportionment Revolution* (New York: Random House, 1966 ed.); see my *Reapportionment* (New York: Scribner's, 1965).

81. 369 U.S. 438 (1962).

82. Cf. *Winterspoon v. Illinois,* 391 U.S. 510 (1968).

83. J.A.C. Grant, "Felix Frankfurter: A Dissenting Opinion," *U.C.L.A. Law Review* 12 (1965): 1037–38; see my "Rhetoric of Constitutional Change," pp. 44–50.

84. See Hugo Lafayette Black, *A Constitutional Faith* (New York: Knopf, 1968), pp. 33–36. For a good example of the *reductio ad absurdum* of a literal mind in action, see Black's dissent in *Berger v. United States,* 388 U.S. 41, 88 (1967), where he argues that the Fourth Amendment "cannot be implied" to preclude wiretapping, because the words "electronic eavesdropping" do not appear in the language of the amendment.

85. *Warren Court,* p. 315; and *Benton v. Maryland,* 395 U.S. 784, 787, 794 (June 23, 1969), overruling *Palko v. Connecticut,* 302 U.S. 319 (1937). Cf. *North Carolina v. Pearce,* 395 U.S. 711 (June 23, 1969).

86. Krislov, *Supreme Court and Political Freedom,* pp. 190–91; James P. Levine, "The Bookseller and the Law of Obscenity; Toward an Empirical Theory of Free Expression" (Ph.D. diss., Northwestern University, 1968).

87. See my *Constitutional Politics,* pp. 636–38.

88. *Warren Court,* pp. 167, 287.

89. *Cameron v. Johnson,* 390 U.S. 611 (1968).

90. *Constitutional Politics,* pp. 653–54.

91. Krislov reports a similar finding that for the 1963 and 1964 terms, and in regard to all claims of "freedom of expression," the Warren Court upheld only 46 per cent of fifty claims against the national government, but 60 per cent of eighty-three claims against state governments. See his *Supreme Court and Political Freedom,* p. 174 Table 5–5.

92. Ibid., pp. 174–75.

93. *Warren Court,* p. 358.

Chapter II. Constitutional Politics

1. As quoted by Charles A. Beard, *The Supreme Court and the Constitution* (Englewood Cliffs: Prentice-Hall, 1962 reprint of 1938 rev. ed.), p. 41.

2. Alpheus T. Mason, *The Supreme Court from Taft to Warren* (Baton Rouge: Louisiana State University Press, 1958), p. 68; C. Herman Pritchett, *Roosevelt Court,* p. 3.

3. *Supreme Court from Taft to Warren*, p. 113.

4. For a discussion of a few of the unfolding possibilities, see Albert D. Biderman and Herbert Zimmer, eds., *The Manipulation of Human Behavior* (New York: Wiley, 1961); James L. Hildebrand, "Soviet International Law: An Exemplar for Optimal Decision Theory Analysis," *Case Western Law Review* 20 (1968): 220–49; Albert Somit, "Toward a More Biologically-Oriented Political Science: Ethology and Psychopharmacology," *Midwest Journal of Political Science* 12 (1968): 550–67; Somit, "Psychopharmacology and Politics: Potential Problems," and James C. Davies, "The Psychobiology of Political Behavior: Some Provocative Developments," papers presented at the 23rd Annual Meeting of the Western Political Science Association (Honolulu, April 4, 1969).

5. According to a Canadian Press news release of April 14, 1969, Douglas, speaking before a pro-Zionist group in Montreal, proclaimed his support for minority protests and civil disobedience, as means for by-passing the communications monopolies because the mass media "are in the hands of a group representing the rich, the vested interests and the establishment"—including "the established political parties [which] are dominated by entrenched authorities."

6. William Howard Taft, *Our Chief Magistrate and His Powers* (New York: Columbia University Press, 1916), pp. 99–102; Daniel S. McHargue, "President Taft's Appointments to the Supreme Court," *Journal of Politics* 12 (1950): 494–95.

7. Alpheus T. Mason, *William Howard Taft: Chief Justice* (New York: Simon and Schuster, 1965), pp. 39–40, 79–80, 87, and especially p. 77.

8. Walter F. Murphy, "In His Own Image: Mr. Chief Justice Taft and Supreme Court Appointments," in Philip B. Kurland, ed., *The Supreme Court Review: 1961* (Chicago: University of Chicago Press, 1961) and "Chief Justice Taft and the Lower Court Bureaucracy: A Study in Judicial Administration," *Journal of Politics* 24 (1962): 453–76.

9. Walter F. Murphy, *The Elements of Judicial Strategy* (Chicago: University of Chicago Press, 1964), Ch. 4; Mason, *William Howard Taft*, Chs. 5 and 9.

10. 285 U.S. xxxiv (1931), as noted in Mason, *William Howard Taft*, p. 223n.

11. David J. Danelski, "The Influence of the Chief Justice in the Decisional Process of the Supreme Court," paper presented at the 59th Annual Meeting of the American Political Science Association (September 1963), p. 20, n. 122. Cf. Alexander M. Bickel, *The Unpublished Opinions of Mr. Justice Brandeis: The Su-*

preme Court at Work (Cambridge: Harvard University, Belknap Press, 1957).

12. One conspicuous exception was *Meyer* v. *Nebraska,* 262 U.S. 390 (1923).

13. As Mason points out, "After having personally conducted [such] hearings he remarked . . . 'Why I had no idea. How can people live on such wages?'" *Supreme Court from Taft to Warren,* p. 51.

14. *Sloan Shipyards Corp.* v. *United States Shipping Board,* 258 U.S. 549, 570 (1922).

15. 261 U.S. 525 (1923).

16. *United Zinc and Chemical Co.* v. *Britt,* 258 U.S. 266, 280 (1922); *United States* v. *Moreland,* 258 U.S. 433, 441 (1922).

17. 262 U.S. 447 (1923).

18. Carl Wittke, "Mr. Justice Clarke—A Supreme Court Judge in Retirement," *Mississippi Valley Historical Review* 36 (1949): 27–50.

19. See Joseph C. Hutcheson, Jr., "The Judgment Intuitive: The Function of the 'Hunch' in Judicial Decision," *Cornell Law Quarterly* 14 (1929): 724–88. Hutcheson was among the half dozen persons whom Roosevelt had considered for the appointment that went to Hugo Black. Joseph Alsop and Turner Catledge, *The 168 Days* (New York: Doubleday, 1938), p. 298.

20. Jack W. Peltason, *Federal Courts in the Political Process* (New York: Doubleday, 1955), p. 16.

21. David J. Danelski, *A Supreme Court Justice is Appointed* (New York: Random House, 1964), Ch. 3.

22. Mason, *William Howard Taft,* p. 213. On McKenna's enforced retirement, see David J. Danelski, "Supreme Court Justice Steps Down." Even Holmes had to be asked by his colleagues to retire: Mason, *The Supreme Court from Taft to Warren* (1968 rev. ed.), p. 229.

23. Danelski, *Supreme Court Justice is Appointed,* Ch. 1; Mason, *William Howard Taft,* Ch. 2; Joel F. Paschal, *Mr. Justice Sutherland: A Man Against the State* (Princeton: Princeton University Press, 1951).

24. Fred Rodell, *Nine Men: A Political History of the Supreme Court of the United States from 1790 to 1955* (New York: Random House, 1955), p. 223; cf. Samuel Handel, *Charles Evans Hughes and the Supreme Court* (New York: Russell and Russell, 1951), p. 67: "Justice Hughes qualifies as one of the foremost, if not the foremost, liberal member of the Court during his initial period of service."

25. John P. Frank, *The Marble Palace* (New York: Knopf,

1958), p. 48; Jack W. Peltason, *Fifty-eight Lonely Men: Southern Federal Judges and School Desegregation* (New York: Harcourt, Brace and World, 1961), p. 22; Rodell, *Nine Men*, p. 222: "that [the Senate was] misguided in blocking Parker was subsequently proved by Parker's outstanding liberal judicial record for more than a quarter of a century after."

26. Rodell, *Nine Men*, p. 223.

27. See my *Quantitative Analysis of Judicial Behavior* (New York: The Free Press of Glencoe, 1959), p. 314.

28. 252 U.S. 416 (1920).

29. Kelly and Harbison, *American Constitution*, pp. 677–78.

30. Mason, *William Howard Taft*, p. 216.

31. 274 U.S. 200, 208 (1927).

32. 302 U.S. 319, 329 (1937).

33. Danelski, *Supreme Court Justice is Appointed*, pp. 160–61, 189–90.

34. 277 U.S. 438, 485 (1928).

35. Danelski, *Supreme Court Justice is Appointed*, pp. 181–83.

36. For evidence of the apparent incongruity between Butler's judicial passion for procedural due process, and his pre-judicial—and it was also prejudicial—behavior as a regent of the University of Minnesota, in the ruthless and hysterical kangaroo-court proceedings against Professor Walter A. Schaper on September 13, 1917, see ibid., pp. 100–03.

37. Pritchett, *Roosevelt Court*, pp. 244–46.

38. See my "Academic Ideology and the Study of Adjudication," *American Political Science Review* 61 (1967): 118.

39. See Fairman, "Retirement of Federal Judges," pp. 406, 417–18, 422–23, 429, 439–40. See also Sidney Ulmer's discussion of "Some Behavioral Postulates" in Joel Grossman and Joseph Tanenhaus, eds., *The Frontiers of Judicial Research* (New York: Wiley, 1969), pp. 339–42.

40. *Roosevelt Court*, pp. 242, 244.

41. Ibid., p. 256.

42. *Korematsu v. United States*, 323 U.S. 214, 219 (1944).

43. *Roosevelt Court*, p. 247.

44. See my *Judicial Mind*, p. 109.

45. See my *Constitutional Politics*, pp. 636–38; cf. C. Herman Pritchett, *Congress versus the Supreme Court, 1957–1960* (Minneapolis: University of Minnesota, 1961), pp. 12–13.

46. *Constitutional Politics*, p. 611; *Wolf v. Colorado*, 338 U.S. 25 (1949).

47. *Monroe v. Pape*, 365 U.S. 167, 202 (1961).

48. Grant, "Felix Frankfurter," p. 1042.

NOTES

49. Harold W. Chase, "Federal Judges: The Appointing Process," *Minnesota Law Review* 51 (1966): 185–221.

50. See, e.g., Anthony Lewis, *Gideon's Trumpet* (New York: Random House, 1964).

51. See Harold P. Spaeth, "Race Relations and the Warren Court," *University of Detroit Law Journal* 43 (1965): 255–72, esp. Fig. 1, p. 270.

52. See, for example, Black's pro-Confederacy remarks in his solitary dissent against the constitutionality of the Voting Rights [for Negroes] Act of 1965, in *Allen* v. *State Board of Elections*, 393 U.S. 544, 595, 597 (March 3, 1969).

53. *Adderley* v. *Florida*, 385 U.S. 39 (1966); *Walker* v. *City of Birmingham*, 388 U.S. 307 (1967).

54. *Constitutional Politics*, pp. 610–11.

55. See Black's illiberal dissent in the birth control clinic decision, *Griswold* v. *Connecticut*, 381 U.S. 479, 507 (1965); cf. his *ex cathedra* attack on his proprivacy brethren, in his Carpentier Lectures at Columbia Law School in 1968, *A Constitutional Faith* (New York: Knopf, 1968), pp. 9–10.

56. *Harper* v. *Virginia Board of Elections*, 383 U.S. 663, 670 (1966); *Texas* v. *United States*, 384 U.S. 155 (1966).

57. *Cox* v. *Louisiana*, 379 U.S. 559, 575 (1965); *Cameron* v. *Mississippi*, 381 U.S. 741, 742 (1965); *Amalgamated Food Employees Union Local 590* v. *Logan Valley Plaza, Inc.*, 391 U.S. 308, 327 (1968).

58. *Tinker* v. *Des Moines Independent Community School District*, 393 U.S. 503, 525 (1969). "This case," he continued, "subjects all the public schools in the country to the whims and caprices of their loudest-mouthed, but maybe not their brightest, students." Idem.

59. See, e.g., his dissenting opinion in *Amalgamated Food Employees Union Local 590* v. *Logan Valley Plaza*, 391 U.S. 308, 332–33 (1968); and his solitary dissent in *Sniadach* v. *Family Finance Corp.*, 395 U.S. 337, 344–51 (1969), against the Court's decision that the Wisconsin wage garnishment statute violated "the fundamental principles of due process."

60. "Race Relations," pp. 270–71. Characterizing the defendants' behavior as "extra-legal" seems to beg the very question at issue.

61. Thereby making "it far more difficult to protect society 'against those who have made it impossible to live today in safety'," as Black put the matter in his dissent in *Harrison* v. *United States*, 392 U.S. 219, 226 (1968).

189

62. *Griffin* v. *Maryland,* 378 U.S. 130, 138 (subsuming 318–46) (June 22, 1964).

63. *Tinker* v. *Des Moines,* 393 U.S. 503 (February 24, 1969).

64. Mr. Justice Sanford, speaking for the majority in *Gitlow* v. *New York,* 268 U.S. 652, 669 (1925).

65. *Constitutional Faith,* p. 64.

66. Ibid., p. 10; cf. pp. xiv and 24.

67. Cf. Joel B. Grossman, "Dissenting Blocs on the Warren Court: A Study in Judicial Role Behavior," *Journal of Politics* 30 (1968): 1068–90, at 1078–79.

68. *Constitutional Faith,* p. 65.

69. Ibid., pp. 45, 54, 63.

70. *Connecticut General Life Insurance Co.* v. *Johnson,* 303 U.S. 77, 85 (1938): "I do not believe the word 'person' in the Fourteenth Amendment includes corporations. . . . I believe this Court should now overrule previous decisions which interpreted the Fourteenth Amendment to include corporations."

71. "Justice Black and the Bill of Rights," *CBS News Special,* CBS Television Network (Tuesday, December 3, 1968), mimeographed transcript (Columbia Broadcasting System, Inc., 1968), p. 8.

72. "I cannot close," he confesses in the Epilogue to his *A Constitutional Faith,* "without saying a few words to express my deep respect and boundless admiration and love for our Constitution and the men who drafted it"; p. 65.

73. *Tinker* v. *Des Moines,* 393 U.S. 503, 524 (1969).

74. *The Supreme Court in the American System of Government* (Cambridge: Harvard University Press, 1955).

75. See my *Dispassionate Justice: A Synthesis of the Judicial Opinions of Robert H. Jackson* (Indianapolis: Bobbs-Merrill, 1969), esp. Chs. 1 and 10; see also the discussion of Black's maximal negative loading on a factorial dimension of radicalism, in my "Simulating the Supreme Court: An Extension of the Tenth Man Game," *Journal of Legal Education* 22:5 (June 1970), in press.

76. Concerning Frankfurter, see Raymond Moley, "A Great Dissent," *Newsweek* 59 (April 16, 1962): 116; and Grant, "Felix Frankfurter." For other views on Black, see Samuel Krislov, "Mr. Justice Black Reopens the Free Speech Debate," *U.C.L.A. Law Review* 11 (1964): 189–211; and Michael Ash, "The Growth of Justice Black's Philosophy on Freedom of Speech: 1962–1966," *Wisconsin Law Review* 1967: 840–62.

NOTES

Chapter III. The American Polity

1. Arnold S. Kaufman, *The Radical Liberal: New Man in American Politics* (New York: Atherton, 1968).

2. See Arthur S. Miller, "Notes on the Concept of the 'Living' Constitution," *George Washington Law Review* 31 (1963): 881–918.

3. See my "The Rhetoric of Constitutional Change."

4. Earl Warren, "The Law and the Future," *Fortune* 52 (November 1955): 107. (I am indebted for this quotation to Walter F. Murphy's *Congress and the Court: A Case Study in the American Political Process* [Chicago: University of Chicago Press, 1962], p. 250.)

5. Dissenting in *Terminiello v. Chicago*, 337 U.S. 1, 32, 33–34 (1949).

6. Vilhelm Aubert, "Chance in Social Affairs," *Inquiry* 2 (1959): 1–24.

7. Mason, *William Howard Taft*, Chs. 4 and 5, esp. pp. 109–14.

8. Felix Frankfurter and James Landis, *The Business of the Supreme Court* (New York: Macmillan, 1927), p. 302, Table 1.

9. Mason, *William Howard Taft*, pp. 133–37.

10. Except for one discussion of public reaction to Roosevelt's Court-packing plan, a subject to which we shall return presently. See Frank V. Cantwell, "Public Opinion and the Legislative Process," *American Political Science Review* 40 (1946): 924–35.

11. This paragraph, and the two that follow it, are based directly upon the data reported in Walter Murphy and Joseph Tanenhaus, "Public Opinion and The United States Supreme Court: A Preliminary Mapping of Some Prerequisites for Court Legitimation of Regime Changes," *Law and Society Review* 2 (1968): 357–84.

12. Ibid., pp. 368, 376.

13. Kenneth M. Dolbeare, "The Public Views the Supreme Court" in Herbert Jacob, ed., *Law, Politics, and the Federal Courts* (Boston: Little, Brown, 1967).

14. Ibid., p. 200.

15. There is one study, based upon a strictly local (and highly biased, in relation to the national population) sample (in Seattle) that reports strong support for both the Court and its pro–civil liberties policies, from a majority of well-informed, well-educated, middle-class, nonpartisan males, and with the also divergent finding that support for the Court was positively correlated with knowledge about it. John Kessel, "Public Perceptions of the Supreme Court," *Midwest Journal of Political Science* 10 (1966): 167–91.

16. Kenneth M. Dolbeare and Phillip E. Hammond, "The Political Party Basis of Attitudes toward the Supreme Court," *Public Opinion Quarterly* 32 (1968): 29.

17. Mason, *William Howard Taft*, pp. 92–93.

18. See my *Constitutional Politics*, p. 712 (chart, "Composition of the Court at the End of the October, 1958, Term").

19. Walter F. Murphy and Joseph Tanenhaus, "Public Opinion and Supreme Court: The Goldwater Campaign," *Public Opinion Quarterly* 32 (1968): 40.

20. Ibid., p. 47.

21. Ibid., p. 33.

22. Ibid., p. 47.

23. See Robert Horn, *Groups and the Constitution* (Stanford: Stanford University, 1956); Clement Vose, *Caucasians Only: The Supreme Court, the NAACP, and the Restrictive Covenant Cases* (Berkeley: University of California, 1959).

24. Mason, *William Howard Taft*, p. 93.

25. Alsop and Catledge, *168 Days*, pp. 116–18, 163–82.

26. Murphy, *Congress and the Court*, pp. 139–41, 251–56.

27. Clifford M. Lytle, *The Warren Court and Its Critics* (Tucson: University of Arizona, 1968), Ch. 4.

28. Lloyd Wells, "The Supreme Court and Public Opinion, 1937–1959," in John Claunch, ed., *The Politics of Judicial Review, 1937–1959* (Dallas: Southern Methodist University Press, 1957), p. 41.

29. John Schmidhauser, *The Supreme Court: Its Politics, Personalities, and Procedures* (New York: Holt, Rinehart and Winston, 1960), p. 81.

30. Ibid., p. 90. On the ABA's lobbying during this era to infiltrate the legislative process, cf. my "Politics and the Constitution: The Bricker Amendment during 1953," *Journal of Politics* 16 (1954): 257–98.

31. Joel B. Grossman, *Lawyers and Judges: The ABA and the Politics of Judicial Selection* (New York: Wiley, 1965), pp. 70–72; cf. Harold W. Chase, "The Johnson Administration: Judicial Appointments, 1963–1966," *Minnesota Law Reveiw* 52 (1968): 965–99.

32. Murphy, *Congress and the Court*, p. 95.

33. These resolutions are reprinted in Pritchett, *Congress versus the Supreme Court*, pp. 137–40.

34. Lytle, *Warren Court*, pp. 98–99.

35. Ibid., p. 100; Grossman, *Lawyers*, p. 75; Murphy, *Congress and the Court*, p. 255n.

36. Jack Peltason, *Fifty-eight Lonely Men*, pp. 7, 117–22; cf.

NOTES

Charles V. Hamilton, "Southern Judges and Negro Voting Rights: The Judicial Approach to the Solution of Controversial Social Problems," *Wisconsin Law Review* 1965: 1–31.

37. Kenneth Vines, "Federal District Judges and Race Relations Cases in the South," *Journal of Politics* 26 (1964): 341–43.

38. Ibid., pp. 346–47.

39. Kenneth Vines, "The Role of Circuit Courts of Appeal in Federal Judicial Process: A Case Study," *Midwest Journal of Political Science* 7 (1961): 310; Vines, "Southern State Supreme Courts and Race Relations," *Western Political Quarterly* 18 (1965): 7.

40. The above paragraph is based upon Vines, "Southern State," pp. 6–7, 9, 10, 17; and G. Theodore Mitau, *Decade of Decision: The Supreme Court and the Constitutional Revolution, 1954–1964* (New York: Scribner's, 1967), pp. 220–21.

41. The resolutions are reprinted in Pritchett, *Congress versus the Supreme Court*, pp. 141–59.

42. Lytle, *Warren Court*, p. 72.

43. Murphy, *Congress and the Court*, pp. 224–25.

44. See my *Constitutional Politics*, pp. 284–94.

45. Murphy, *Congress and the Court*, p. 152.

46. Ibid., Chs. 8 and 9, and p. 249; Pritchett, *Congress versus the Supreme Court*, passim.

47. Cantwell, "Public Opinion"; Murphy, *Congress and the Court*, p. 61.

48. Murphy, *Congress and the Court*, pp. 117, 213, 226.

49. Chester A. Newland, "Legal Periodicals and the United States Supreme Court," *Midwest Journal of Political Science* 3 (1959): 60–64.

50. "Legislative Apportionment and the Federal Courts," *Harvard Law Review* 71 (1958): 1057–98.

51. *Brief for the United States as Amicus Curiae on Reargument of Baker v. Carr, Appellate Docket No. 6, October Term 1961.*

52. 369 U.S. 186 (1962).

53. *Hartford Co. v. Harrison*, 301 U.S. 459 (1937).

54. *Vitarelli v. Seaton*, 359 U.S. 535 (1959).

55. Murphy, *Congress and the Court*, p. 251.

56. Ibid., p. 123.

57. Ibid., p. 231.

58. Murphy and Tanenhaus, "Public Opinion and the U.S. Supreme Court: A Preliminary Mapping," p. 362, and "Public Opinion and Supreme Court: The Goldwater Campaign," p. 36; cf. Mitau, *Decade*, p. 7.

59. Murphy and Tanenhaus, "Public Opinion and the U.S. Supreme Court: A Preliminary Mapping," p. 358.

60. See my *Reapportionment*, pp. 139–40.

61. Murphy, *Congress and the Court*, p. 264.

62. Dolbeare, "Public Views," p. 206.

63. Murphy and Tanenhaus, "Public Opinion and Supreme Court: The Goldwater Campaign," p. 36.

64. *Decade*, pp. 66–70.

65. See the special issue on "Affirmative Integration: Studies of Efforts to Overcome De Facto Segregation in the Public Schools," *Law and Society Review* 2 (November 1967).

66. Mitau, *Decade*, p. 78.

67. Ibid., pp. 199–200.

68. Ibid., pp. 233–34.

69. Ibid., pp. 120–21.

70. H. Frank Way, Jr., "Survey Research on Judicial Decisions: The Prayer and Bible Reading Cases," *Western Political Quarterly* 21 (1968): 204.

71. This statement, and the preceding part of this paragraph, are based upon Chester A. Newland, "Press Coverage of the United States Supreme Court," *Western Political Quarterly* 17 (1964): 28–30.

72. Richard M. Johnson, *The Dynamics of Compliance: Supreme Court Decision-Making from a New Perspective* (Evanston: Northwestern University Press, 1967), p. 83.

73. Ibid., p. 88.

74. Ibid., p. 90.

75. See Mitau, *Decade*, pp. 134–41.

76. Ibid., p. 141.

77. "Survey Research," pp. 189–205.

78. See Kenneth Dolbeare and Phillip Hammond, "Local Elites, the Impact of Judicial Decisions, and the Process of Change" (paper read at the 65th annual meeting of the American Political Science Association; New York, N.Y., September 3, 1969).

79. Ibid., p. 195.

80. Ibid., p. 199.

81. Ibid., p. 204.

82. Mitau, *Decade*, pp. 145–46.

83. Richard M. Johnson, "Compliance and Supreme Court Decision-Making," *Wisconsin Law Review* (1967): 174.

84. Cf. William K. Muir, Jr., *Prayer in the Public Schools: Law and Attitude Change* (Chicago: University of Chicago, 1967), an in-depth study of cross pressures upon a small sample of the educational-elite decision makers in a single school district in a large eastern city.

85. Mitau, *Decade*, pp. 5, 7, 187.

NOTES

86. *United States* v. *Wade,* 388 U.S. 218 (1967).

87. Mitau, *Decade,* p. 161.

88. Delmar Karlen, *Anglo-American Criminal Justice* (New York: Oxford University Press, 1967), pp. 42, 44.

89. Abraham S. Blumberg, "The Practice of Law as a Confidence Game: Organizational Cooptation of a Profession," *Law and Society Review* (1967): 39.

90. Abraham Blumberg, *Criminal Justice* (Chicago: Quadrangle Books, 1967).

91. See Arthur L. Wood, *Criminal Lawyer* (New Haven: College and University Press, 1967).

92. Blumberg, "Practice," p. 37.

93. Newland, "Press," p. 29.

94. Mitau, *Decade,* pp. 103–10.

95. Ibid., p. 96.

96. Ira H. Carmen, *Movies, Censorship and Law* (Ann Arbor: University of Michigan Press, 1967); Levine, "The Bookseller."